POPCORN!

100 A-MAIZE-ING POPCORN RECIPES
TO MAKE AT HOME

POPCORN!

100 A-MAIZE-ING POPCORN RECIPES TO MAKE AT HOME

CAROL BECKERMAN

APPLE

A Quintet Book

First published in the UK in 2013 by
Apple Press
74-77 White Lion Street
London N1 9PF
United Kingdom

www.apple-press.com

ISBN: 978-1-84543-495-3
QTT.POPC

This book was conceived, designed, and produced by
Quintet Publishing Limited
4th Floor, Sheridan House
114-116 Western Road
Hove BN3 1DD
United Kingdom

Project Editor: Ross Fulton
Designer: Allen Boe, listeningbear.com
Photographer: Adrian Lawrence
Food Stylist: Sue Henderson
Art Director: Michael Charles
Editorial Director: Donna Gregory
Publisher: Mark Searle

Manufactured in China by 1010 Printing International Ltd.

10 9 8 7 6 5 4

CONTENTS

INTRODUCTION

A SHORT HISTORY OF POPCORN

Popcorn has been eaten as a snack in the United States for thousands of years – the oldest ears of popcorn to have been found are believed to be at least 4,000 years old. They were discovered in the Bat Cave of west-central New Mexico in 1948 and 1950, and ranged from smaller than a penny to about 5 cm (2 in) in size.

Early Native Americans grew corn, which they called 'mahiz' (which evolved into the more familiar 'maize'), and they introduced it to the English who went to America in the 16th and 17th centuries. It is believed that Native Americans discovered that corn kernels popped when thrown into a fire or hot sand. Popcorn was not only an important food at the time, but was also used by Native Americans and Aztec Indians to make garlands worn by women at celebration dances.

After the introduction of the mouldboard plow in the US in the mid-1800s, corn growing became more widespread and led to an increase in the popularity of popping corn as a recreational activity. Popcorn was sold at carnivals and circuses, as well as in the grocery stores. With the invention of 'talking pictures', cinemas initially refused to sell popcorn because it was too messy, so their customers took in their own popcorn, purchased from street sellers. The cinemas soon caught on and introduced their own concession stands to provide the snack.

During the Great Depression, popcorn was one of the few luxuries that the average man in the street could afford, being relatively cheap at five or ten cents a bag. While many other businesses failed, the popcorn business thrived. When America entered World War II, sugar was sent overseas for US troops, so sweets became scarce, and Americans ate three times as much popcorn as usual. Later, as television became popular, there was a small slump in popcorn consumption, as Americans deserted the cinemas to stay home in front of the TV; but soon, snacking while watching television increased the consumption of popcorn again.

The popularity of this snack has grown and grown, and today it is one of America's most enduring and popular snacks. People of all ages love popcorn, and the statistics prove it: Americans consume about 65 billion litres (114 billion pints) of popped popcorn each year.

POPPING IS FUN

You start off with so little, and end up with so much! Just 100 g (3.5 oz) of unpopped kernels produces two generous servings of popcorn, seemingly from nowhere.

The smell of popcorn popping is one that excites the senses of young and old alike, and makes the mouth water for a large bowlful. Just about everything is better enjoyed with popcorn, and almost everyone loves it. TV programmes become more of an event, movies are more exciting, and if you want to make instant friends, make a batch of popcorn and walk through a crowded room! It is one of the most beloved snacks of all time. But how does it pop?

In very simple terms, corn kernels pop because the outer hull is hard, and the inside of the kernel contains starch and moisture. As the corn kernel is heated, steam is produced inside the hull by the moisture, and when it has built up enough pressure it explodes and bursts through the hull, expanding as it does so, producing popcorn. A few kernels will be left unpopped after heating; these are referred to as 'old maids'. Always remove them carefully, making sure you get every last one. Your family, your friends and your teeth will thank you.

Once your popcorn is popped, there are many ways to enjoy it. Completely plain, without butter, salt or sugar, it is a very healthy snack – low-fat, low-calorie and low-sugar. Add a little olive oil and savoury spices, herbs and seasonings and you still have a reasonably healthy snack, because good (mainly unsaturated) fats are not that bad for you. When you start adding ingredients such as butter, sugar and chocolate, the calorie and fat and sugar content will shoot up, but it is so worth it!

You can grind popped popcorn kernels down to make your own maize flour, either fine or coarse. You can add this to muffins or brownies, or coat chicken and fish fillets. You can also make your own tortillas. One of the main benefits of this use of popcorn is that it resembles breadcrumbs, but without the gluten, so it's ideal for those with wheat and gluten intolerances. Also, if you need breadcrumbs and have none, but have popcorn in your kitchen cabinets – use that instead.

POPPING TECHNIQUES

Popcorn can be popped in several ways — in the microwave, on the hob, in a halogen oven, or in an electric air popper made specifically for popcorn. Avoid using a normal domestic oven as it simply does not work. Different methods of popping yield slightly different amounts of popcorn.

For most of these recipes the amount of popcorn used is 100 g (3.5 oz) unpopped popcorn kernels, which produces enough popcorn for 2 medium servings, but this measurement is not critical.

If you are going to enjoy your popcorn with just salt and butter, add the salt to the popcorn kernels before you start cooking (except if using an air popper), and add the butter afterwards. If you are going to follow one of the recipes in this book, leave out the salt and butter when cooking the popcorn.

MICROWAVE METHOD

This should be done in a food-safe, microwave-safe paper bag. Brown paper bags are generally not recommended. If you are going to follow one of the recipes in this book, follow this recipe twice to make a large enough amount, and leave out the seasoning.

50 g (1¾ oz) popcorn kernels
½ teaspoon olive oil
½ teaspoon salt

Place the popcorn in the paper bag and add the olive oil and salt. Fold the top of the bag over twice, and stand the bag upright if possible in the microwave. If it will not stand up, lay it on its side. Cook on high until you hear the popping slow to a couple of pops a second. Remove the bag from the microwave. Be careful as you open the bag as it will be full of steam. Pour the popcorn into a medium-sized bowl, taste and adjust the seasoning if necessary.

HOB METHOD

To pop the corn on the hob, you will need a covered saucepan and an oil with a high smoking point. The best ones to use are vegetable, olive, coconut, peanut, or grapeseed. Do not use butter as it may burn.

3 tablespoons oil
75 g (2¾ oz) popcorn kernels

A 3-litre (5-pint) saucepan is a good size for 75 g (2¾ oz) of kernels. Add the oil to the pan and set it on medium-high heat. Put 3 or 4 popcorn kernels into the oil and cover the pan. When the kernels pop, add the rest of the popcorn kernels in an even layer. Sprinkle with salt. Cover, remove from heat, and count 30 seconds. This step first heats the oil to the right temperature, and waiting 30 seconds brings all of the other kernels to a near-popping temperature, so that when they are put back on the heat, they all pop at about the same time.

Return the pan to the heat. The popcorn should begin popping soon, and all at once. Once the popping starts in earnest, gently shake the pan by moving it back and forth over the burner. Try to keep the lid slightly ajar to let the steam from the popcorn escape (the popcorn will be drier and crisper). Once the popping slows to several seconds between pops, remove the pan from the heat, remove the lid, and pour the popcorn into a bowl.

With this method, nearly all of the kernels should pop, and none should burn.

HALOGEN OVEN METHOD

75 g (2¾ oz) popcorn kernels

Preheat the halogen oven to 250° C (480° F). Spread the popcorn kernels on the oven tray in one even layer. Cook on the low shelf of the oven for 8 minutes, then let the popcorn rest in the oven for 5 minutes to ensure all the corn has popped. There will still be a few kernels that do not pop. Remove from the oven and pour into a bowl.

AIR POPPER METHOD

75 g (2¾ oz) popcorn kernels

This is the easiest method of popping. Follow the manufacturer's instructions, and you will have popcorn in seconds. The machine should pour the popped corn into a large bowl placed strategically in front, but one of the disadvantages is that the machine can sometimes send the popped corn flying in all directions. Hold a tea towel in front of the machine if this happens, and direct the flow back into the bowl.

USING POPCORN IN RECIPES

Popped popcorn kernels are quite delicate. When mixing them with other ingredients, be very careful that you do not break up the popcorn. You'll need to mix popped popcorn with other ingredients for many of the recipes found in this book. Always use a large bowl – you need quite a bit of room to turn the mixture over without it going everywhere.

Before combining ingredients, lightly oil the mixing bowl as well as the wooden spoon or spatula before you start. This makes mixing easier. This is particularly useful when mixing popcorn with a sugar syrup or caramel. Another tip is to warm the bowl and keep the popcorn warm in the oven at a low heat before adding sugar syrups or caramel. This helps to prevent hardening, which makes it very difficult to stir in the popcorn. The same method applies when making popcorn balls, so oil or butter your hands to help prevent sticking.

Some of the recipes in this book call for finishing popcorn by baking in the oven. This is usually with olive oil or butter, and has the effect of making the popcorn crispier and improving coverage and flavor. When pressing the popcorn recipes into baking pans, it will be easier if you use something to press down the mixture, such as an oiled potato masher, waxed paper, buttered hands, or the oiled back of a wooden spoon.

When storing your popcorn creations, use an airtight container. Popcorn usually keeps quite well for up to a week, but do not store popcorn in the refrigerator as this will soften it. If your popcorn does become soft, you can refresh it in the oven: Spread it out on a cookie sheet and cook for 5 minutes at 130° C (250° F, gas mark 1/2).

INGREDIENTS

Most of the ingredients used in this book are available in your local supermarket. The exceptions are the edible gold dust and the decorating sugar, which are available wherever cake decorating supplies are sold.

Some people have preferred types or brands of popcorn. I don't. When I tested these recipes, I used a variety of popcorn brands and the end result was always good.

The butter used in the recipes is salted, unless stated otherwise.

Sugar is granulated, unless stated otherwise.

Seasoning is very much down to personal preference. Coarse sea salt has larger flakes and gives a fuller flavour on the tongue, whereas popcorn salt is fine and will be more evenly distributed throughout the popcorn.

OTHER INGREDIENTS

SUGAR SYRUPS AND CARAMEL

When using a sugar thermometer to make a sugar syrup or caramel, if possible clip it to the side of the pan rather than resting it on the bottom of the saucepan, which might give a false reading. During the making of caramel, do not stir while the sugar syrup is approaching the required temperature. After that temperature is reached, it is referred to as caramel.

COCONUT

To toast sweetened shredded coconut for a recipe, spread the coconut out in a single layer on a metal baking tray. Bake for 3 to 5 minutes at 180° C (350° F, gas mark 4) watching closely so that the coconut doesn't burn. Remove from the oven as soon as the coconut is a light golden brown, and set aside to cool.

TOASTED AND ROASTED NUTS

To toast or roast nuts for a recipe, spread out the nuts in a single layer on a metal baking pan. Bake for about 10 to 15 minutes at 180° C (350° F, gas mark 4), watching carefully so that they do not burn, and stirring occasionally, until they are golden brown. Remove from the oven and set aside to cool. Nuts can also be toasted in a dry frying pan over medium heat. Cook and stir until they are golden brown, about 5 minutes. Set aside to cool.

CHOCOLATE

To melt chocolate, place it in a heatproof bowl over a pan of barely simmering water. Make sure that the bottom of the bowl does not touch the water. Leave until just melted. Remove from the heat and stir gently until smooth. Either use immediately or set aside to cool slightly, as necessary.

PAPER CONES FOR ICING

To make a nonstick baking paper cone for icing or drizzling chocolate, fold over a 20 x 30 cm (8 x 12-in) sheet of nonstick baking or greaseproof paper diagonally, then cut the paper with scissors along the crease to create two triangles. Roll one of the triangles into a cone shape and either staple it in place or fold the tail end into the cone on the seam side. Fill the cone with icing, or chocolate, and fold in the corners of the cone, making sure you fold the top down again before beginning to pipe. Snip off the point of the cone with scissors. The size of the opening determines how thick you want the line of icing to be. Keep the other paper triangle to make another cone.

ESSENTIAL EQUIPMENT

Not all recipes will require the equipment listed below, but for the more complicated recipes I have assumed that you will have these items to hand.

Large roasting tins
Baking trays
Cake tins
Wooden spoon or rubber spatula
Whisk
Sugar thermometer
Various sizes of glass bowls and serving bowls
Large saucepan with a lid
Nonstick baking paper

A NOTE ON PHOTOGRAPHY

On pages featuring two recipes, the recipe at the top of the page will be featured in the facing photograph.

Chapter 1

SNACKS
AND APPETISERS

GARLIC AND THYME POPCORN WITH BLACK PEPPER

Start the preparation for this snack 48 hours before you need it, as the popcorn kernels are soaked in garlic-infused oil before being popped in a pan on the hob.

INGREDIENTS
- 240 ml (8 fl oz) extra virgin olive oil
- 100 g (3.5 oz) unpopped popcorn kernels
- 2 cloves garlic, peeled and crushed
- 8 sprigs fresh thyme
- 1½ teaspoons salt
- 2 teaspoons freshly ground black pepper
- 2 teaspoons garlic powder
- 2 tablespoons fresh thyme leaves, stalks removed

METHOD
Heat the oil in a medium pan over medium heat for about 3 minutes. Remove from the heat, transfer to a medium bowl, and add the popcorn kernels, garlic, thyme sprigs and 1 teaspoon salt. Cover and allow to stand at room temperature for 48 hours.

Drain the popcorn kernels through a fine sieve, reserving the oil. Discard the garlic and thyme. Take out 3 tablespoons of the oil and add it with the kernels to a large pan with a lid. Heat over a high heat, lid on, for about 4 minutes, shaking the pan often, until the popping slows down to 2 or 3 pops every few seconds. Remove from the heat and leave for 2 minutes until the popping stops. Transfer the popcorn to a large bowl, and add the remaining salt, black pepper, garlic powder, fresh thyme and 4 to 5 tablespoons of the remaining oil. Stir carefully until well blended. Serve immediately or allow to cool. May be stored for up to 5 days.

Makes 2 medium servings.

ROSEMARY POPCORN WITH PINE NUTS

*The preparation of this popcorn is started 48 hours in advance to make
a wonderful rosemary oil. It is then baked in the oven for about 15 minutes,
sending a wonderful aroma of rosemary around the house.*

INGREDIENTS

- 240 ml (8 fl oz) extra virgin olive oil
- 100 g (3.5 oz) unpopped popcorn kernels
- 10 15-cm (6-in) rosemary sprigs, cut into 5-cm (2-in) pieces
- 1½ teaspoons salt
- 60 g (2 oz) pine nuts
- 2 tablespoons coarsely chopped fresh rosemary leaves

METHOD

Heat the oil in a medium pan over medium heat for about 3 minutes. Remove from the heat, transfer to a medium bowl, and add the popcorn kernels, rosemary sprigs and 1 teaspoon salt. Cover and allow to stand at room temperature for 48 hours.

Preheat the oven to 140° C (275° F, gas mark 1). Drain the popcorn kernels through a fine sieve, reserving the oil. Discard the rosemary. Take 3 tablespoons of the oil and add it with the kernels to a large pan with a lid. Heat over a high heat, lid on, for about 4 minutes, shaking the pan often, until the popping slows down to 2 or 3 pops every few seconds. Remove from the heat and leave for 2 minutes until the popping has stopped. Transfer the popcorn to a large bowl and add the remaining salt, pine nuts, chopped rosemary and 4 to 5 tablespoons of the remaining oil. Stir carefully until well blended. Spread on 1 or 2 large baking trays and bake in the oven for about 15 minutes. Serve immediately while still warm.

Makes 2 medium servings.

LEMON BASIL BUTTERED POPCORN

*Lemon and basil are a classic combination and make a delicious popcorn – though if
you wish, you can use lemon and black pepper seasoning instead of fresh lemon rind.*

INGREDIENTS

- 75 g (2¾ oz) butter
- 2 teaspoons dried basil
- 1 teaspoon lemon zest
- 2 servings popped popcorn
- ½ teaspoon salt

METHOD

In a small pan, melt the butter over low heat. Add the basil and grated lemon rind and stir to combine. Remove from the heat and allow to cool slightly.

Preheat the oven to 140° C (275° F, gas mark 1). Place the popped popcorn in a large bowl, add the butter mixture, and stir or toss gently to combine. Spread on 1 or 2 large baking trays and bake in the oven for 15 minutes. Remove from the oven and sprinkle with salt. Serve warm or allow to cool before serving.

Makes 2 medium servings.

PECORINO POPCORN WITH GARLIC OLIVE OIL

*Pecorino cheese is a salty Italian cheese made from ewe's milk. It is
a hard cheese, often used for grating, and ideal for adding to popcorn.*

INGREDIENTS

- 2 tablespoons extra virgin olive oil
- 3 cloves garlic, peeled and crushed
- 2 servings popped popcorn
- 50 g (1¾ oz) finely grated pecorino cheese
- ½ teaspoon salt
- Freshly ground black pepper

METHOD

Heat the oil and garlic in a small pan over medium heat for
5 minutes. Remove from the heat, cover and allow to stand for
1 to 12 hours to infuse. After infusing, warm the oil again over
medium heat, then discard the garlic.

Preheat the oven to 140° C (275° F, gas mark 1). Place the popped
popcorn in a large bowl, add the oil, cheese, salt and pepper. Stir
gently to combine. Spread on 1 or 2 large baking trays and bake in
the oven for 15 minutes. Remove from the oven and serve warm
or cooled.

Makes 2 medium servings.

TIP

Cheese lovers can experiment with pecorino Romano
(sharp and salty), pecorino Toscano (milder, creamy)
and other regional pecorino varieties.

MAMA'S ITALIAN POPCORN

*This wonderful mixture of Italian herbs and garlic, spiced up with
dried chilli flakes, also can be used as a dip for Italian bread, with a ratio
of 2 teaspoons of herb mix to 3 tablespoons of extra virgin olive oil.*

INGREDIENTS

- 75 g (2¾ oz) butter or margarine
- 1 teaspoon crushed dried chilli flakes
- 1 teaspoon freshly ground black pepper
- 1 teaspoon dried oregano
- 1 teaspoon dried rosemary
- 1 teaspoon dried basil
- 1 teaspoon dried parsley
- 1 teaspoon garlic powder
- 1 teaspoon salt
- 2 servings popped popcorn

METHOD

In a small pan, melt the butter or margarine over low heat. Add the dried chilli flakes, pepper, herbs, garlic powder, and salt, and stir to combine. Remove from the heat and allow to cool slightly.

Preheat the oven to 140° C (275° F, gas mark 1). Place the popped popcorn in a large bowl, add the seasoned butter, and stir or toss gently to combine. Spread on 1 or 2 large baking trays and bake in the oven for 15 minutes. Serve warm from the oven or allow to cool before serving.

Makes 2 medium servings.

TIP

You may well want to tweak the ratios of herbs and spices in this recipe, but make sure to keep the balance of herby, salty and spicy!

SUN-DRIED TOMATO AND BASIL POPCORN

Bright sun-dried tomatoes and fresh basil leaves not only give a splash of colour to this popcorn, but also add a fresh, tangy flavour.

INGREDIENTS

- 3 tablespoons vegetable oil
- 100 g (3.5 oz) unpopped popcorn kernels
- 2 cloves garlic, peeled and crushed
- 1½ tablespoons olive oil
- 50 g (1¾ oz) finely grated Parmesan cheese
- ½ teaspoon salt
- Handful fresh basil leaves, finely chopped
- 6 sun-dried tomatoes in oil, drained and finely chopped
- 1 tablespoon oil from the tomatoes

METHOD

Preheat the oven to 130° C (250° F, gas mark 1/2).

Put the vegetable oil, popcorn kernels and garlic in a large pan with a lid. Heat the pan, lid on, over high heat for about 4 minutes, shaking the pan often, until the popping slows down to 2 or 3 pops every few seconds. Remove from the heat and leave for 2 minutes until the popping has stopped. Transfer the popcorn to a large bowl, remove the garlic, and add the olive oil, cheese, salt, basil, tomatoes and tomato oil. Stir or toss gently to combine. Transfer to 1 or 2 large baking trays and bake in the oven for about 40 minutes. Serve warm from the oven or allow to cool before serving.

Makes 2 medium servings.

TIP

Sun-dried tomatoes work well with many different herbs, such as parsley or oregano, as well as garlic or cheeses – why not experiment?

CARIBBEAN SPICED POPCORN

This zesty mix of Caribbean flavours can be easily tweaked
according to your personal taste.

INGREDIENTS

For the Caribbean spice mix:
- 2 tablespoons ground turmeric
- 1 tablespoon ground coriander
- 1½ teaspoons ground cumin
- 1½ teaspoons ground cinnamon
- 1 teaspoon ground ginger
- 1 teaspoon garlic powder
- ½ teaspoon freshly ground black pepper
- ¼ teaspoon ground cloves

- 3 tablespoons melted butter
  or butter-flavoured oil spray
- 2 servings hot popped popcorn
- Coarse sea salt, to taste

METHOD

First make the Caribbean spice mix by combining all the spices in a medium bowl.

Either brush the sides of a large serving bowl with a little melted butter, or spray with butter-flavoured oil. Add 3 or 4 cups of hot popped popcorn to the bowl, spray lightly or sprinkle with a little melted butter, and sprinkle with one quarter of the seasoning mix and coarse sea salt, to taste. Repeat three times until all the popcorn and all the seasoning have been layered in the bowl. Serve immediately, without tossing.

Makes 2 medium servings.

TIP

Caribbean cuisine encompasses an incredible number of flavours which have come together from many different cultures. To add to the fusion, toss in to the mix some fried plantains, chickpeas or some freeze-dried tropical fruit.

COUNTY FAIR KETTLE CORN

This recipe was inspired by my daughter telling me about the fabulous sweet and salty kettle corn she tried at the Santa-Cali-Gon Days Festival in Independence, Missouri. She said it was so good that folks were buying bags of it as big as their children. This recipe won't make quite that much.

INGREDIENTS
- 100 g (3.5 oz) unpopped popcorn kernels
- 3 tablespoons vegetable oil
- 50 g (1¾ oz) white sugar
- 1 teaspoon salt, or to taste

METHOD

In a large pan with a lid, place the popcorn kernels and oil, cover, and heat over high heat, shaking the pan frequently. Watch carefully, and when you hear the first kernel pop, remove the pan from the heat. Carefully and quickly remove the lid and add the sugar. Stir and replace the lid. Put the pan back onto the high heat and, shaking frequently, wait until the popping slows to 2 or 3 pops every few seconds. Remove the pan from the heat and leave for 2 minutes until the popping has stopped. Transfer the hot popcorn to a large serving bowl, add salt to taste, and toss to combine. Serve immediately or allow to cool before serving.

Makes 2 medium servings.

QUICK CAJUN POPCORN

This is very fast to throw together at the last minute if you fancy a little spice with your popcorn.

INGREDIENTS
- 2 servings popped popcorn
- 60 ml (2 fl oz) extra virgin olive oil
- 1 tablespoon paprika
- 1 teaspoon dried thyme
- 1 teaspoon garlic powder
- ½ teaspoon crushed dried chilli flakes
- salt to taste

METHOD

Place the popcorn in a large serving bowl.

In a small pan, heat the oil over medium heat for 3 to 4 minutes. Add the paprika, thyme, garlic powder, crushed dried chilli flakes and salt, and stir to combine. Pour mixture over the popped corn and stir or toss together gently until well mixed.

Makes 2 medium servings.

CURRIED POPCORN

Why not excite your taste buds before an Indian curry with popcorn spiced with garam masala and turmeric?

INGREDIENTS

- 2 servings popped popcorn
- 4 tablespoons butter
- 2 teaspoons garam masala
- 2 teaspoons ground turmeric
- ½ teaspoon chilli powder
- Salt
- Freshly ground black pepper

METHOD

Preheat the oven to 140° C (275° F, gas mark 1).

Place the popcorn in a large serving bowl.

In a small pan, melt the butter, then add the garam masala, turmeric and chilli powder. Stir mixture over a gentle heat for 3 to 4 minutes, remove from the heat, and pour over the popcorn. Add salt and pepper to taste and stir or toss gently to combine. Transfer popcorn to 1 or 2 large baking trays and bake in the oven for 15 minutes. Serve while hot or allow to cool before serving.

Makes 2 medium servings.

TIP

Cashew nuts can often be found in Indian cuisine – try adding 75 g (2¾ oz) to the popcorn before baking, and adding 85 g (3 oz) raisins after baking.

PESTO POPCORN

This pesto is delicious and quick to make, as it is blended in a food processor. You could also use it on pasta. Stored in a jar with a little olive oil poured on top to seal it, the pesto will keep for a week or so in the refrigerator.

INGREDIENTS

For the pesto:
- 40 g (1½ oz) pine nuts
- Large bunch fresh basil leaves
- 35 g (1¼ oz) finely grated Parmesan cheese
- 35 g (1¼ oz) finely grated pecorino cheese
- 150 ml (5 fl oz) extra virgin olive oil, plus extra for storing the pesto
- 1 clove garlic, chopped

- 2 servings popped popcorn

METHOD

To make the pesto, toast the pine nuts in a small dry frying pan over medium heat until lightly coloured. Set aside to cool. Put the cooled pine nuts, basil, cheeses, 150 ml (5 fl oz) olive oil, and garlic in a food processor. Pulse together until combined, but try not to overprocess. You do not want it to be a mush. Alternatively you could use a pestle and mortar, which, although it will take longer and be harder work, will give a better texture and a brighter colour.

Place the popcorn in a large serving bowl. Add 6 to 8 tablespoons of the pesto and toss gently to combine. Serve immediately.

Cover and store any leftover pesto in the refrigerator, and use within 1 week.

Makes 2 medium servings.

SESAME SOY POPCORN

This popcorn has an exotic and very distinctive flavour, with the use of sesame oil, sesame seeds and soy sauce.

INGREDIENTS

- 2 servings popped popcorn
- 175 g (6 oz) glucose syrup
- 1 tablespoon sesame oil
- 60 ml (2 fl oz) soy sauce or light soy sauce
- 25 g (1 oz) sesame seeds

METHOD

Place the popcorn in a large serving bowl.

In a small pan, heat the glucose syrup, sesame oil and soy sauce over a medium heat. Bring the mixture to a boil, lower the heat, and simmer gently for 5 minutes, stirring occasionally. Remove the pan from the heat and pour the mixture over the popcorn. Sprinkle on the sesame seeds and toss gently to combine. Best served warm.

Makes 2 medium servings.

HICKORY SMOKIN' BARBECUE CRACKER POPCORN

Most people love the flavour of barbecue. If you can find small cheese biscuits,
add them to the popcorn for extra crunch and texture.

INGREDIENTS

- 2 servings popped popcorn
- 2 teaspoons onion powder
- 2 teaspoons paprika
- 1½ teaspoons chilli powder, or to taste
- 1 teaspoon lemon pepper seasoning
- 1 teaspoon salt
- 1 teaspoon garlic powder
- ½ teaspoon mustard powder
- 120 g (4 oz) butter
- 1 teaspoon hickory smoke flavour
- 175 g (6 oz) small cheese biscuits (optional)

METHOD

Place the popcorn in a large serving bowl. Preheat the oven to 140° C (275° F, gas mark 1).

In a medium bowl, mix together onion powder, paprika, chilli powder, lemon pepper, salt, garlic powder and mustard powder. Set aside.

In a small pan over a gentle heat, melt the butter, add the hickory smoke flavour, and stir to combine. Remove from the heat and pour over the popcorn. Sprinkle on the seasoning mix and toss gently until well combined. Spread on 1 or 2 large baking trays and bake in the oven for 15 minutes. Remove from the oven and transfer to a large serving bowl. Add the crackers, if using, mix together, and serve immediately or allow to cool before serving. May be stored for up to 4 days.

Makes 2 medium servings.

SCARBOROUGH FAIR POPCORN

This popcorn has been named after the song made famous by Simon and Garfunkel
and, of course, includes the herbs parsley, sage, rosemary and thyme. The lemon juice
cuts through the herbs and lifts the flavour out of the ordinary.

INGREDIENTS

- 2 servings popped popcorn
- 4 tablespoons butter
- 1 teaspoon dried parsley flakes
- ¼ teaspoon powdered dried sage
- ½ teaspoon crushed dried rosemary
- 1 teaspoon dried thyme leaves
- ½ teaspoon lemon juice
- ½ teaspoon salt, or to taste

METHOD

Place the popcorn in a large serving bowl.

In a medium pan, melt the butter over a gentle heat. Add the herbs and lemon juice and stir to combine. Pour over the popcorn, add salt to taste, and toss gently until evenly distributed. Serve immediately or allow to cool.

Makes 2 medium servings.

BLACK TRUFFLE OIL POPCORN

This sophisticated, aromatic, tasty popcorn is a sure bet to impress,
as it is drizzled with truffle oil.

INGREDIENTS

- 2 servings popped popcorn
- 50 g (1¾ oz) finely grated Parmesan cheese
- 1 teaspoon freshly ground black pepper
- 2 tablespoons black truffle oil
- ½ teaspoon salt

METHOD

Place the popcorn in a large bowl, add the Parmesan cheese and black pepper, and toss gently to combine. Drizzle with the truffle oil and salt, and toss again, until well mixed. Sprinkle with salt, and serve immediately.

Makes 2 medium servings.

SWISS, BACON AND ONION POPCORN

This combination is always a favourite, especially when used to flavour popcorn.

INGREDIENTS

- 2 servings popped popcorn
- 225 g (8 oz) bacon, chopped
- 1 medium onion, finely chopped
- 60 g (2 oz) finely grated Swiss cheese
- 1 teaspoon freshly ground black pepper

METHOD

Preheat the oven to 150° C (300° F, gas mark 2). Place the popcorn in a large bowl.

In a large frying pan over medium-high heat, sauté the bacon and onion until the bacon is crisp and the onion is softened. Pour the bacon, onion and 3 tablespoons bacon fat over the popcorn. Add the cheese and black pepper and toss gently to combine. Spread on 1 or 2 large baking trays and bake in the oven for 7 to 8 minutes, until the cheese has melted. Serve immediately.

Makes 2 medium servings.

SPICY CHILLI AND LIME POPCORN

This popcorn has a tang from fresh lime, a slight kick from chilli powder, and a lovely crunch from pine nuts and flaked almonds.

INGREDIENTS

- 2 servings popped popcorn
- 3 tablespoons butter or margarine
- 120 g (4 oz) pine nuts
- 50 g (1¾ oz) flaked almonds
- 1 teaspoon chilli powder
- ½ teaspoon salt
- ½ teaspoon grated lime rind
- 1 tablespoon freshly squeezed lime juice
- ½ teaspoon ground cumin
- ½ teaspoon freshly ground black pepper

METHOD

Place the popcorn in a large serving bowl.

Preheat oven to 140° C (275° F, gas mark 1). In a medium pan, melt the butter or margarine over medium heat, then add the pine nuts, almonds, chilli powder, salt, lime rind and juice, ground cumin and pepper. Cook mixture for 3 to 4 minutes, and pour it over the popcorn. Toss gently to combine. Spread popcorn on 1 or 2 large baking trays and bake in the oven for 15 minutes. Serve warm from the oven or allow to cool before serving.

Makes 2 medium servings.

BAYOU POPCORN

This seasoning mix is reminiscent of the bayou flavours of Louisiana.
It could also be used as a flavouring for chicken or steak.

INGREDIENTS

For the bayou seasoning mix:
- 3 tablespoons paprika
- 1 tablespoon garlic powder
- 2 teaspoons onion powder
- 2 teaspoons brown sugar
- 1½ teaspoons crushed dried chilli flakes
- 1 teaspoon dried thyme
- 1 teaspoon dried oregano
- 1 teaspoon freshly ground black pepper
- ½ teaspoon ground nutmeg

- 2 servings popped popcorn
- 120 g (4 oz) butter
- ½ teaspoon salt, or to taste

METHOD

To make the bayou seasoning, in a medium bowl, mix together the paprika, garlic powder, onion powder, brown sugar, dried chilli flakes, thyme, oregano, black pepper and nutmeg. The mixture can be stored in an airtight container and used within 1 month.

Preheat the oven to 180° C (350° F, gas mark 4). Place the popcorn in a large serving bowl.

In a small pan, over a gentle heat, melt the butter and pour it over the popcorn. Sprinkle on about 2 tablespoons bayou seasoning mix, add salt to taste, and toss gently until evenly distributed. Spread popcorn on 1 or 2 large baking trays and bake in the oven for 15 minutes. Either serve warm or allow to cool before serving. The popcorn can be stored for up to 3 days.

Makes 2 medium servings.

TIP

Try adding 1 teaspoon fennel seeds and 1 teaspoon ground cinnamon to the spices. As Cajun cooking is synonymous with 'heat with flavour', you could also add a pinch of cayenne pepper.

PAD THAI POPCORN

This is an amazing popcorn. The caramel base makes it sweet and crunchy, and the lime and fish sauce make it spicy and aromatic. Coriander provides the final flourish.

INGREDIENTS

- 2 servings popped corn
- 175 g (6 oz) dry-roasted peanuts
- 25 g (1 oz) freshly chopped coriander, to serve
- 1 to 2 teaspoons dried red chilli flakes, to serve

For the caramel sauce:

- 175 g (6 oz) brown sugar
- 120 ml (4 fl oz) extra virgin olive oil
- 175 g (6 oz) golden syrup
- 4 to 5 teaspoons freshly squeezed lime juice
- 2 tablespoons lime zest
- 2 teaspoons Asian fish sauce
- 2 tablespoons chilli sauce
- 1 teaspoon garlic powder
- ½ teaspoon bicarbonate of soda

METHOD

Preheat the oven to 130° C (250° F, gas mark 1/2). Place the popcorn in a large bowl and add the peanuts.

To make the caramel sauce, in a large saucepan, mix together the brown sugar, olive oil, corn syrup and lime juice. Bring to a boil over medium-high heat. Boil for 5 minutes, remove from the heat, and add the lime zest, fish sauce, chilli sauce, garlic powder and bicarbonate of soda.

Pour sauce over the popcorn and toss gently to combine. Spread on 1 or 2 large baking trays and bake in the oven for 45 minutes, stirring 3 or 4 times during cooking. Remove from the oven and allow to cool.

To serve, place the popcorn in a large serving bowl, add the coriander and dried chilli flakes, and toss gently to combine before serving.

Makes 2 medium servings.

TIP

For added texture, add some crispy noodles to the popcorn just before serving, at the same time as the coriander and dried chilli flakes.

PEPPERONI POPCORN

*Toasted pumpkin seeds and cashew nuts add extra crunch and texture
to this spicy pepperoni popcorn.*

INGREDIENTS
- 2 servings popped popcorn
- 100g (3½ oz) pumpkin seeds
- 135 g (4½ oz) whole cashew nuts
- 85 g (3 oz) pepperoni, thinly sliced,
  then each slice halved
- 2 teaspoons chilli powder
- 1 teaspoon ground cumin
- Freshly ground black pepper

METHOD
Place the popcorn in a large serving bowl.

In a large dry frying pan, over a gentle heat, lightly toast the pumpkin seeds and cashew nuts, then transfer to a bowl and set aside. Add the pepperoni to the frying pan and dry-fry until crispy. Add to the popcorn with the pumpkin seeds and cashews, chilli powder, ground cumin and black pepper. Toss gently to combine, and either serve immediately or store for up to 2 days.

Makes 2 medium servings.

CANDIED CHEDDAR POPCORN

*Cheddar cheese is melted into caramel and stirred into the popcorn before baking,
ensuring that the cheese is evenly distributed. This popcorn snack has a wonderful
sweet and salty cheesy flavour.*

INGREDIENTS
- 2 servings popped popcorn
- ½ teaspoon coarse sea salt
- ¼ teaspoon cayenne pepper
- 300 g (10½ oz) granulated sugar
- 2 tablespoons maple syrup
- 60 ml (2 fl oz) double cream
- 120 g (4 oz) grated cheddar cheese

METHOD
Preheat the oven to 150° C (300° F, gas mark 2). Spread the popcorn in a very large roasting pan. Sprinkle with the salt and cayenne pepper and toss gently to combine.

In a large saucepan over low to medium heat, stir together the sugar and maple syrup with 60 ml (2 fl oz) water, and heat until the sugar has dissolved. Increase the heat and bring to a boil. Keep boiling until the syrup turns a deep amber colour, about 10 minutes or so. Remove from the heat and add the cream, being careful as the mixture will bubble up. Add the grated cheddar cheese, stir quickly until the cheese has melted, and pour mixture over the popcorn. Stir with a wooden spoon until evenly distributed. Bake in the oven for 45 minutes. Stir several times during cooking to coat the popcorn completely with the caramel and cheese. Remove from the oven and serve immediately or allow to cool before serving.

Makes 2 medium servings.

TEX-MEX POPCORN

Tex-Mex ingredients were probably some of the first fusion flavours invented, influenced not only by colourful Mexican food but also by the pioneers and settlers in Texas.

INGREDIENTS
- A little butter for greasing
- 2 servings popped popcorn
- 1 tablespoon paprika
- 1 tablespoon dried oregano
- 1 tablespoon ground cumin
- 1 teaspoon salt
- ½ teaspoon onion powder
- ½ teaspoon garlic powder
- ¼ teaspoon cayenne pepper
- 120 ml (4 fl oz) extra virgin olive oil
- 1 tablespoon freshly chopped coriander

METHOD
Preheat the oven to 140° C (275° F, gas mark 1), and lightly grease 1 or 2 large baking trays with a little butter. Put the popcorn into a large bowl.

In a small bowl, mix the paprika, oregano, cumin, salt, onion powder, garlic powder and cayenne pepper together, and set aside. In a medium pan, heat the oil over a gentle heat. Pour the oil over the popcorn, add the herb and spice mixture, and toss gently to combine. Spread on the baking trays and bake in the oven for 15 minutes. Remove from the oven, add the chopped coriander, and toss to combine. Serve immediately.

Makes 2 medium servings.

TIP
The flavours in this recipe are all classic Tex-Mex. Adding 200 g (7 oz) pitted black olives to the mixture along with the coriander will contribute to its authenticity.

COOL RANCH POPCORN

If you like a cool ranch salad dressing or dip, you're sure to like this popcorn.

INGREDIENTS

- 2 servings popped popcorn
- 75 g (2¾ oz) butter
- 1 tablespoon buttermilk powder
- 2 teaspoons dried parsley flakes
- 1 teaspoon onion powder
- 1 teaspoon garlic salt
- ½ teaspoon chilli powder
- ¼ teaspoon dried dill

METHOD

Place the popcorn in a large bowl. In a small pan, melt the butter over a gentle heat. In a medium bowl, mix together the buttermilk powder, parsley flakes, onion powder, garlic salt, chilli powder and dill. Add mixture to the butter in the pan, stir, and pour over the popcorn. Stir or toss gently to combine. Allow to cool before serving. May be stored for up to 4 days.

Makes 2 medium servings.

CURRIED PARMESAN POPCORN

Using store-bought curry powder makes this popcorn snack very quick to prepare.

INGREDIENTS

- 2 servings popped popcorn
- 75 g (2¾ oz) butter or margarine
- 50 g (1¾ oz) finely grated Parmesan cheese
- ½ teaspoon salt
- 1 teaspoon curry powder
- 1 teaspoon dried coriander leaves
- 1 teaspoon freshly ground black pepper

METHOD

Place the popcorn in a large serving bowl. In a small pan, over a gentle heat, melt the butter or margarine. Allow to cool slightly, then pour over the popcorn. Add the cheese, salt, curry powder, dried coriander leaves and black pepper. Toss gently to combine, and either serve immediately or store for up to 5 days.

Makes 2 medium servings.

BACON CARAMEL POPCORN

Who can resist bacon or caramel? Blend them together with tasty cashew nuts, and the result is irresistible.

INGREDIENTS

- 2 servings popped popcorn
- 8 rashers of bacon
- ½ teaspoon coarse sea salt
- ¼ teaspoon cayenne pepper
- 60 g (2 oz) whole cashews
- 300 g (10½ oz) granulated sugar
- 60 ml (2 fl oz) water
- 2 tablespoons maple syrup
- 60 ml (2 fl oz) double cream

METHOD

Preheat the oven to 150° C (300° F, gas mark 2). Spread the popcorn over the base of a very large roasting pan.

In a large frying pan over medium-high heat, cook the bacon until crispy, drain on paper towels, and crumble when cooled. Sprinkle the salt and cayenne pepper over the popcorn, and toss gently to combine. Scatter the bacon and cashews over the top.

In a large saucepan over low to medium heat, stir together the sugar and maple syrup with 60 ml (2 fl oz) water, and heat until the sugar has dissolved. Increase the heat and bring to a boil. Keep boiling until the syrup turns a deep amber colour, about 10 minutes or so. Remove from the heat and add the cream, being careful as the mixture will bubble up. Stir quickly until blended, then pour over the popcorn. Stir with a wooden spoon or spatula until evenly distributed, and bake in the oven for 45 minutes. Stir several times during cooking to coat the popcorn completely with the caramel. Remove from the oven and allow to cool completely before serving.

Makes 2 medium servings.

TIP

Bacon is not the only meat you could use for this recipe – try substituting pepperoni or chorizo for a tasty change.

SWEET AND SALTY SEAWEED EXPLOSION

Seaweed, often used in Japanese cooking, has an amazingly versatile flavour that adds a new dimension to popcorn. This recipe will wow your friends and family with your innovative flair. Look for nori furikake in the Asian section of your supermarket.

INGREDIENTS
- 2 servings popped popcorn
- 75 g (2¾ oz) butter
  or 75 ml (3 fl oz) vegetable oil
- 3 tablespoons nori furikake
- 1 tablespoon honey
- 1 teaspoon salt

METHOD
Place the popcorn in a large serving bowl. In a medium saucepan, melt the butter or heat the oil over a gentle heat until warmed, then pour over the popcorn. Add 2 tablespoons nori furikake and toss gently to combine. Add another tablespoon of nori furikake and toss again until evenly distributed. Add the honey in a thin zigzag drizzle to avoid making sticky clumps, and season carefully with a little salt. Stir carefully and taste to get it right. No one flavour should overpower another. You should be able to taste all the flavours – the salt, the sweet honey and the nori furikake – at once.

Makes 2 medium servings.

TIP
You could also use dried nori seaweed in a risotto, combined with pearl barley, finely chopped spinach and a blend of your favourite cheeses.

SMOKY MESQUITE POPCORN

You can buy smoky mesquite flavouring on its own, but it is so much more satisfying to add your own combination of spices, and so much tastier.

INGREDIENTS

For the mesquite flavouring mix:
- 1 teaspoon brown sugar
- 2 tablespoons smoked paprika
- 1 teaspoon ground cumin
- 1 teaspoon salt
- ½ teaspoon garlic powder
- ½ teaspoon onion powder
- ½ teaspoon ground chipotle pepper
- ½ teaspoon crushed dried rosemary
- ½ teaspoon dried marjoram
- ½ teaspoon mesquite smoke flavouring
- ¼ teaspoon dried sage leaves
- ⅛ teaspoon freshly ground black pepper
- ⅛ teaspoon mustard powder

- 2 servings popped popcorn
- 120 g (4 oz) butter

METHOD

Preheat the oven to 140° C (275° F, gas mark 1).

In a medium bowl, mix the brown sugar with all the herbs and spices, stirring to combine well.

Place the popcorn in a large bowl. In a medium pan, over a gentle heat, melt the butter, then pour it over the popcorn. Add the seasoning mixture and toss gently to combine. Spread the popcorn on 1 or 2 large baking trays and bake in the oven for 15 minutes. Serve immediately or allow to cool before serving.

Makes 2 medium servings.

PERI PERI POPCORN

Peri peri flavour originated in Portuguese colonies in African countries. It is a wonderfully lively and versatile seasoning. You can make it as mild or as hot and spicy as you wish, by adjusting the amount of crushed dried chilli flakes to taste.

INGREDIENTS

For the peri peri mix:
- 2 teaspoons crushed dried chilli flakes
- 2 teaspoons paprika
- 2 teaspoons garlic powder
- 2 teaspoons lemon pepper seasoning
- 2 teaspoons crushed dried rosemary
- 1 teaspoon dried oregano
- 1 teaspoon salt

- 2 tablespoons butter
- 2 servings popped popcorn
- 50 g (1¾ oz) flaked almonds

METHOD

Preheat the oven to 140° C (275° F, gas mark 1).

To make the peri peri seasoning mix, in a small bowl, mix together the crushed dried chilli flakes, paprika, garlic powder, lemon pepper seasoning, rosemary, oregano and salt. Set aside.

In a small pan, over a gentle heat, melt the butter. Place the popcorn in a large bowl. In a small dry frying pan, lightly toast the flaked almonds and add them to the popcorn. Pour the melted butter over the popcorn and almonds, add the peri peri seasoning mix, and toss gently to combine. Spread the popcorn on 1 or 2 large baking trays and bake in the oven for 10 minutes. Serve warm from the oven or allow to cool before serving.

Makes 2 medium servings.

WASABI POPCORN

This is only for the brave, as it is quite hot and spicy.

INGREDIENTS

- 1 teaspoon sugar
- 1 teaspoon salt
- 1 teaspoon wasabi powder, sifted
- ⅛ teaspoon cayenne pepper
- 2 tablespoons butter
- 2 servings popped popcorn

METHOD

In a small bowl, mix together the sugar, salt, wasabi powder and cayenne pepper. Set aside. In a small pan, melt the butter over a low heat. Place the popcorn in a large serving bowl, add the butter and the wasabi mixture, and toss gently to combine before serving.

Makes 2 medium servings.

BLACK PEPPER AND PARMESAN POPCORN

Sometimes just one or two flavours added to plain popcorn is enough. Black pepper and Parmesan complement each other so perfectly, nothing else is needed.

INGREDIENTS

- 2 servings popped popcorn
- 75 g (2¾ oz) butter
- 150 g (5½ oz) grated Parmesan cheese
- 2 teaspoons freshly ground black pepper

METHOD

Place the popcorn in a large bowl.

Preheat the oven to 170° C (325° F, gas mark 3). In a small pan, melt the butter over a gentle heat. Pour butter over the popcorn, sprinkle with Parmesan cheese and freshly ground black pepper, and toss gently to combine. Spread the popcorn on 1 or 2 large baking trays and bake for 10 minutes. Serve immediately.

Makes 2 medium servings.

Chapter 2

BALLS AND BARS

It is easy to form popcorn into balls or to make bars in a baking tray, which elevate popcorn into an easy-to-transport snack. From savoury garlic and cheese balls to power bars, there's something here to please everyone.

CHOCOLATE PEANUT BUTTER BARS

Chocolate and peanut butter together are a magical combination.
These bars make a great addition to a lunch box.

INGREDIENTS
- 75 g (2¾ oz) butter, plus extra for greasing
- ⅔ serving popped popcorn
- 175 g (6 oz) plain chocolate chips
- 175 g (6 oz) golden raisins
- 135 g (4½ oz) smooth peanut butter
- 300 g (10½ oz) miniature marshmallows

METHOD
Grease a 18 x 28-cm (7 x 11-in) baking tray with a little butter.
Place the popcorn, chocolate chips and raisins in a large bowl.

In a medium pan, melt the remaining butter over a gentle heat
and stir in the peanut butter. Add the marshmallows and stir
continuously until melted. Remove from the heat and pour over
the popcorn, mixing quickly with a buttered wooden spoon or
spatula until combined. Transfer mixture to the buttered baking
tray, press into the edges, and smooth the top. Allow to cool
before cutting into bars. Either serve immediately or store
for up to 4 days.

Makes 8 bars.

TIP
For a change, substitute white chocolate chips for plain, and
dried cherries for the golden raisins. You could even throw in
some roughly chopped peanuts for extra crunch.

SWEET AND SPICY PUMPKIN AND POPCORN BALLS

Full of delicious Autumnal flavours, these balls are the perfect treat for after school snacks and chilly evenings.

INGREDIENTS

- 2 servings popped popcorn
- 300 g (10½ oz) hulled natural pumpkin seeds (not roasted or salted)
- 300 g (10½ oz) sugar
- 250 g (9 oz) glucose syrup
- 350 ml (12 fl oz) double cream
- 3 tablespoons unsalted butter, cut into small pieces, plus extra for forming balls
- ½ teaspoon salt
- 2 teaspoons vanilla extract
- 1 teaspoon ground cinnamon
- ½ teaspoon cayenne pepper

METHOD

Line two large baking trays with nonstick baking paper. Place the popcorn into a large bowl.

In a large dry frying pan over medium heat, toast the pumpkin seeds, stirring, until lightly browned and starting to pop. Do this in batches to avoid crowding the pan. Add the seeds to the popcorn.

In a large pan over a gentle heat, cook the sugar and glucose syrup, stirring occasionally, until the sugar has dissolved. Increase the heat to medium-high and bring sugar syrup to a boil. Cook until a sugar thermometer registers 140° C (275° F), about 6 minutes. Meanwhile, warm the cream in a small pan over a gentle heat, and keep warm. When the sugar syrup has reached the desired temperature, whisk in the butter and salt. Gradually pour in the cream and vanilla, being careful because the mixture will bubble up. Reduce the heat and continue to simmer, stirring occasionally, until the syrup registers 115° C (240° F). Remove from the heat immediately and add the cinnamon and cayenne pepper. Cool for 2 minutes, then pour the syrup over the popcorn and pumpkin seeds. Stir gently to combine, then set the mixture aside until it is cool enough to handle.

Butter your hands and shape the mixture into 5-cm (2-in) balls, placing them on the prepared baking trays. Serve at room temperature, or wrap individually in cling film and store for up to one week.

Makes about 50 balls.

TIP

For extra spice and flavour, add a few cardamom seeds. Take 3 cardamom pods, crush them and carefully remove the little black seeds with the tip of a knife.

POPCORN S'MORES BARS

*American children love s'mores bars of any type. Popcorn makes these
extra special so give them a try.*

INGREDIENTS
- 150 g (5½ oz) butter, plus extra for greasing
- 2 servings popcorn, popped using the hob method (page 7)
- 300 g (10½ oz) miniature marshmallows
- 225 g (8 oz) roughly broken rich tea biscuits
- 225 g (8 oz) plain chocolate chips
- 215 g (7½ oz) brown sugar
- 225 g (8 oz) glucose syrup
- 1 teaspoon bicarbonate of soda

METHOD
Lightly butter a 23 x 33-cm (9 x 13-in) baking tray. Place the popcorn in a large bowl, and add the marshmallows, rich tea biscuits and chocolate chips. Stir to combine.

In a large saucepan, over a gentle heat, cook together the sugar, 150 g (5½ oz) butter, and corn syrup, stirring frequently, until the sugar has dissolved. Increase the heat to medium-high and cook for 5 minutes, without stirring. Remove the pan from the heat, immediately add the bicarbonate of soda, and stir to combine. Be careful, as the mixture will bubble up. Pour the butter mixture over the popcorn mix, and stir gently until the popcorn is evenly coated. Transfer the mixture to the buttered baking tray, press into the edges, and smooth the top. Leave until cooled completely, before cutting into 24 bars.

Makes 24 bars.

LITTLE APPLE POPCORN BALLS

These balls are packed with the goodness of apples, flavoured with spices, brown sugar, and syrup. They are excellent to accompany a picnic for energy.

INGREDIENTS

- 2 servings popped popcorn
- 1 cup roughly chopped toasted walnuts (see page 9)
- 1 cup roughly chopped dried apples
- 2 tablespoons butter, plus extra for forming balls
- 2 tablespoons granulated sugar
- 2 tablespoons brown sugar
- 30 ml (1 fl oz) black treacle
- 30 ml (1 fl oz) golden syrup
- 90 g (3¼ oz) glucose syrup
- ½ teaspoon ground cinnamon
- ½ teaspoon ground ginger

METHOD

Line two large baking trays with nonstick baking paper. Place the popcorn in a large bowl. Add the walnuts and dried apples and stir to combine.

In a large pan, melt 2 tablespoons butter over a gentle heat. Add the granulated sugar, brown sugar, black treacle, golden syrup, glucose syrup, cinnamon and ginger, and stir until the sugar has dissolved. Increase the heat to medium-high and bring to a boil. Boil until the temperature has reached 140° C (280° F) on a sugar thermometer. Remove from the heat and quickly pour over the popcorn, stirring to combine. Allow to cool slightly, until cool enough to handle, and form into 30 balls with buttered hands. Place balls on the paper-lined baking trays to cool completely. Wrap the cooled balls individually in cling film. They can be stored for up to 1 week.

Makes 30 balls.

TROPICAL POPCORN BALLS

Coconut and macadamia nuts give a tropical flavour to these delicious creamy balls, which are held together with honey and almond butter. They are best eaten the day they are made.

INGREDIENTS

- 2 servings popped popcorn
- 60 g (2 oz) finely chopped macadamia nuts
- 175 g (6 oz) honey
- 135 g (4½ oz) almond butter
- A little butter for forming balls
- 40 g (1½ oz) sweetened flaked coconut

METHOD

Line two large baking trays with nonstick baking paper. Place popcorn in a large bowl, add the macadamia nuts, and stir to combine.

In a medium pan, over a gentle heat, warm the honey and almond butter for a few minutes, stirring continuously, until the butter has melted. Increase the heat to medium-high and bring to a boil. Continue to stir for 1 minute, remove from the heat, and quickly pour the almond butter mixture over the popcorn mix. Stir gently with a wooden spoon to combine.

Smear your hands with butter, and working quickly, press the popcorn mixture into balls about 5-cm (2-in) in diameter. Place the balls on the paper-lined baking trays. Sprinkle with flaked coconut while still damp and sticky, turning the balls around to cover all over. Allow to cool. Either serve immediately or wrap individually in cling film and store for no more than 2 days.

Makes about 50 balls.

PRETZEL AND PEANUT POPCORN BARS

Salty and sweet, these bars are a wonderful after-school snack for children. They are substantial and filling and will keep them going until teatime.

INGREDIENTS
- A little butter for greasing
- 1½ servings popped popcorn
- 300 g (10½ oz) coarsely chopped salted pretzels
- 120 g (4 oz) salted peanuts
- 50 g (1¾ oz) coarsely chopped pecans
- 400g (13¾ oz) sugar
- 1 teaspoon salt, plus extra for sprinkling
- 150 ml (5 fl oz) double cream
- 100 g (3½ oz) miniature marshmallows

METHOD
Lightly grease a 30 x 30-cm (12 x 12-in) baking tray with butter.

Place popcorn, pretzels, peanuts and pecans in a large bowl, and stir to combine. Set aside. In a medium pan, over a gentle heat, dissolve the sugar in 110 ml (3¾ fl oz) water with 1 teaspoon salt. Increase the heat to medium-high and bring to a boil. Continue to boil, without stirring, until the syrup turns an amber colour, about 6 minutes. Remove from the heat and carefully add the cream; the mixture will bubble up. Immediately add the marshmallows and stir until melted.

Pour the syrup over the popcorn mixture and stir until all the pieces are evenly coated with caramel. Transfer the mixture to the baking tray, press into the edges, and smooth the top. Sprinkle with a little extra salt. Leave until cooled completely, before cutting into 24 bars. Store for up to 4 days.

Makes 24 bars.

GRANOLA POPCORN BARS

If you do not have time for breakfast, these delicious granola and popcorn bars are a great substitute to eat on the go.

INGREDIENTS
- 4 tablespoons butter or margarine, plus extra for greasing
- 85 g (3 oz) brown sugar
- 175 g (6 oz) glucose syrup
- 200 g (7 oz) granola
- ½ serving popped popcorn
- 60 g (2 oz) golden raisins
- 120 g (4 oz) coarsely chopped pecans

METHOD
Lightly grease a 23 x 33-cm (9 x 13-in) baking tray with butter.

In a large pan, over a gentle heat, combine the brown sugar, glucose syrup and 4 tablespoons butter. Cook until the butter has melted and the sugar has dissolved. Increase the heat to medium-high and bring to a boil, stirring continuously. Add the granola and popcorn, and stir until well combined. Stir in the raisins and pecans, remove from the heat, and allow to cool for 2 or 3 minutes. Transfer the mixture to the baking tray, press into the edges, and smooth the top. Leave until cooled completely, before cutting into 10 bars. Store for up to 4 days.

Makes 10 bars.

SESAME GINGER POPCORN BALLS

If you like the taste of ginger, you will love these popcorn balls. They're super to serve at Halloween, and they're also wonderful as an appetiser.

INGREDIENTS
- 50 g (1¾ oz) sesame seeds
- 2 servings popped popcorn
- 60 g (2 oz) brown sugar
- 175 g (6 oz) glucose syrup
- 75 g (2¾ oz) butter, plus extra for forming
- 2 teaspoons ground ginger
- 85 8 (3 oz) chopped crystallised ginger

METHOD
Line 2 large baking trays with nonstick baking paper.

In a large dry frying pan, toast the sesame seeds over a gentle to medium heat. Watch them carefully so that they do not burn. Remove from the heat.

Place the popcorn in a large bowl. In a large pan, over a gentle heat, melt together the brown sugar, corn syrup, 75 g (2¾ oz) butter and ground ginger, stirring frequently, until the sugar has dissolved. Increase the heat to medium-high and bring to a boil. Boil until the syrup darkens, about 3 to 4 minutes. Pour the syrup over the popcorn and gently stir until the popcorn is evenly covered. Stir in the crystallised ginger.

Butter your hands and pressing firmly, quickly form the popcorn mixture into 5-cm (2-in) balls. Place them on the paper-lined baking trays. Sprinkle the balls with the toasted sesame seeds, turning them to evenly coat all over. Set aside to cool. To store, individually wrap each ball in cling film. Can be stored for up to 5 days.

Makes about 40 balls.

MARSHMALLOW POPCORN BALLS

These balls are very similar to crispy rice treats. Quick and easy to make with marshmallows, they are sweet, crispy and chewy all at the same time.

INGREDIENTS
- 120 g (4 oz) butter, plus extra for greasing and forming
- 2 servings popped popcorn
- 250 g (9 oz) miniature marshmallows

METHOD
Line two large baking trays with nonstick baking paper. Lightly grease a large bowl with a little butter, and place the popcorn in the bowl.

In a large pan, over a gentle heat, melt 120 g (4 oz) butter. Add the marshmallows and stir to combine until the marshmallows have melted. Remove mixture from the heat and pour it over the popcorn, stirring quickly to combine evenly. Allow to cool slightly. Smear butter on your hands, then form the popcorn into about 30 balls, placing them on the paper-lined trays. Either serve immediately or store for up to 4 days.

Makes about 30 balls.

CHOCOLATE-GLAZED POPCORN SQUARES

Popcorn is mixed with crispy rice cereal and chocolate and peanut butter, then pressed into a square baking tray, covered with a rich chocolate glaze, and cut into squares.

INGREDIENTS
- A little butter for greasing
- 2 servings popped popcorn
- 50 g (1¾ oz) crispy rice cereal
- 200 g (7 oz) granulated sugar
- 350 g (12 oz) glucose syrup
- 85 g (3 oz) smooth peanut butter
- 175 g (6 oz) milk chocolate chips

For the chocolate glaze:
- 4 tablespoons butter
- 3 tablespoons full-fat milk
- 2 tablespoons cocoa powder, sifted
- 280 g (10 oz) icing sugar, sifted

METHOD
Lightly butter a 30 x 30-cm (12 x 12-in) baking tray. Place the popcorn and crispy rice cereal in a large bowl.

In a large pan over a gentle heat, warm the sugar and glucose syrup together, stirring frequently, until the sugar has dissolved. Increase the heat to medium-high and bring to a boil. Add the peanut butter and milk chocolate chips, and stir until well mixed. Remove from the heat and pour over the popcorn and rice cereal. Mix together quickly, then transfer the mixture to the buttered baking tray, press into the edges, and smooth the top. Set aside to cool completely.

To make the glaze, in a small pan over a gentle heat, melt the butter with the milk, add the cocoa powder and icing sugar, and stir together quickly, using a wooden spoon. Keep stirring until the glaze is smooth and glossy. Cool slightly, then smooth over the cooled popcorn in the tray. Leave until cooled completely before cutting into 16 squares. Store for up to 4 days.

Makes 20 squares.

CURRY COCONUT POPCORN BALLS

Influenced by Indian flavours, these are an easy, spicy-but-sweet treat for those with an adventurous spirit.

INGREDIENTS
- 225 g (8 oz) butter, cut into small pieces, plus extra for greasing and forming
- 2 servings popped popcorn
- 175 g (6 oz) sweetened flaked coconut
- 85 g (3 oz) finely chopped candied ginger
- 400 g (13¾ oz) granulated sugar
- 225 g (8 oz) glucose syrup
- 2 teaspoons distilled white vinegar
- 1 tablespoon salt
- 1½ tablespoons curry powder
- 1 teaspoon ground cumin
- ½ teaspoon vanilla extract

METHOD
Line 2 large baking trays with nonstick baking paper.

Lightly butter a large bowl. Place the popcorn in the bowl with the coconut and candied ginger and stir to combine.

In a large pan, place the sugar, glucose syrup, water, vinegar, salt and 150 ml (5 fl oz) water. Stir to combine and cook over a gentle heat until the sugar has dissolved. Increase the heat to medium-high, bring to a boil, and cook until a sugar thermometer registers 135° C (260° F), about 6 minutes. Remove from the heat and add 225 g (8 oz) butter, curry powder, cumin and vanilla. Stir to combine. Quickly pour mixture over the popcorn, and carefully stir with a wooden spoon until the popcorn is thoroughly coated and cool enough to handle.

Butter your hands and form the popcorn into about 30 balls. Place on the paper-lined baking trays and allow to cool completely. Wrap the cooled balls individually in cling film. They can be stored for up to 1 week.

Makes about 30 balls.

GARLIC CHEDDAR POPCORN BALLS

The amount of garlic in this recipe seems extraordinary, but it really works. These little savoury treats are wonderful as an appetiser or as a snack.

INGREDIENTS

- 4 bulbs garlic
- 2 teaspoons salt
- 450 g (14 oz) grated Cheddar cheese
- 1 teaspoon ground cumin
- ½ teaspoon cayenne pepper
- 2 servings popped popcorn
- A little butter for forming

METHOD

Line 2 large baking trays with nonstick baking paper.

Peel the garlic and mince it finely with the salt. This prevents it sticking and also releases the garlic juices. Mix the garlic with the cheese, cumin and cayenne pepper. In a large microwave-safe bowl, layer the popcorn with the cheese mixture, making sure that the cheese is spread evenly through the popcorn. Place the bowl in the microwave, cover with pierced cling film, and cook on high for 1 minute. Give the bowl a shake, and if your microwave does not have a turntable, turn the bowl 180 degrees. Cook for 1 minute more, being careful not to let it burn. Remove from the microwave. Leave to cool slightly until easier to handle, and with buttered hands, quickly form the mixture into 5-cm (2-in) balls. Place on the paper-lined baking trays to cool. Either serve immediately or store for up to 4 days.

Makes about 40 balls.

POPCORN POWER BALLS

These balls are packed full of nuts and granola and flavoured with spices, brown sugar and syrup. After school, after a workout, or at a picnic, they will be sure to keep you bursting with energy.

INGREDIENTS

- 2 servings popped popcorn
- 120 g (4 oz) roughly chopped and toasted walnuts (page 9)
- 50 g (1¾ oz) granola
- 2 tablespoons butter, plus extra for forming
- 2 tablespoons granulated sugar
- 2 tablespoons brown sugar
- 30 ml (1 fl oz) black treacle
- 30 ml (1 fl oz) golden syrup
- 90 g (3¼ oz) glucose syrup
- ½ teaspoon ground cinnamon
- ½ teaspoon ground ginger

METHOD

Line 2 large baking trays with nonstick baking paper.

Place the popcorn in a large bowl. Add the walnuts and granola and mix to combine.

In a large pan, melt the butter over a gentle heat. Add the granulated sugar, brown sugar, treacle, golden syrup, glucose syrup, cinnamon and ginger, and heat, stirring frequently, until the sugar has dissolved. Increase the heat to medium-high and bring to a boil. Boil until the temperature reaches 140° C (280° F) on a sugar thermometer. Remove from the heat and quickly pour the syrup over the popcorn, gently stirring to combine.

Butter your hands and shape the popcorn into 7.5-cm (3-in) balls. Place them on the paper-lined baking trays to cool completely. Either serve immediately, or wrap them individually in cling film and store for up to 1 week.

Makes about 40 balls.

COCOA POP FUDGE SQUARES

The caramel for this recipe is made with condensed milk, which gives such an intense, creamy fudge flavour, you will find you will never have made enough.

INGREDIENTS

- 4 tablespoons butter, plus extra for greasing
- 175 g (6 oz) plain chocolate chips
- 600 g (1 lb 5 oz) granulated sugar
- 240 ml (8 fl oz) condensed milk
- 1 teaspoon salt
- 2 teaspoons vanilla extract
- 1 serving popped popcorn

METHOD

Lightly grease an 20 x 20-cm (8 x 8-in) baking tray with a little butter.

In a large pan, over a gentle heat, melt the chocolate chips. Add the sugar, condensed milk, remaining butter, salt and 340 ml (11½ fl oz) water. Cook until the sugar has dissolved, stirring continuously. Increase the heat to medium-high and bring to a boil. Boil until a sugar thermometer registers 110° C (230° F). Remove from the heat, add the vanilla, and stir to combine. Add the popcorn and toss gently until well coated. Transfer the mixture to the tray, press into the edges, and smooth the top. Leave until cooled completely, then cut into 9 squares. Can be stored for up to 4 days.

Makes 9 squares.

PINK POPCORN BARS

This recipe works brilliantly with any food colouring. Substituting different coloured M&Ms for the cranberries, try orange and black for Halloween and red and green for Christmas. It is very sweet, so keep the portions small.

INGREDIENTS
- 4 tablespoons butter, plus extra for greasing
- 100 g (3½ oz) miniature marshmallows
- 60 ml (2 fl oz) honey
- Few drops red food colouring
- ⅔ servings popped popcorn
- 350 g (12 oz) dried cranberries
- 1 teaspoon salt, for sprinkling

METHOD
Lightly grease a 23 x 33-cm (9 x 13-in) baking tray with a little butter.

In a large pan over a gentle heat, melt the marshmallows, remaining butter, and honey together, stirring continuously. When the mixture is smooth, remove from the heat and stir in a few drops of food colouring until you achieve a colour that suits you. Stir in the popped corn and cranberries and mix thoroughly.

Transfer the mixture to the buttered tray, press into the edges, and smooth the top. Sprinkle with salt. Leave until cooled completely, before cutting into 24 bars. Store for up to 4 days.

Makes 24 bars.

MAPLE CORN SQUARES

This recipe is similar to caramel corn but with the distinctive flavour of maple syrup to enhance the sweetness. Pecans add texture and an extra dimension.

INGREDIENTS
- A little butter for greasing
- 1⅓ servings popped popcorn
- 120 g (4 oz) coarsely chopped pecans
- 240 ml (8 fl oz) maple syrup
- 175 g (6 oz) brown sugar

METHOD
Lightly grease an 20 x 20-cm (8 x 8-in) baking tray with butter. Place the popcorn in a large bowl. Add the pecans and stir to combine.

In a heavy pan, heat the maple syrup and brown sugar with 60 ml (2 fl oz) water over a gentle heat until the sugar has dissolved. Increase the heat to medium-high and bring to a boil. Boil until the syrup reaches 112° C (230° F) on a sugar thermometer. Remove syrup from the heat, pour over the popcorn, and stir gently until evenly coated. Transfer the mixture to the baking tray, press into the edges, and smooth the top. Leave until cooled completely, before cutting into 9 squares. Either serve immediately or store for up to 4 days.

Makes 9 squares.

WHISKY CHOCOLATE POPCORN BALLS

For the grown-ups only, this is one seriously sophisticated snack. The nutty flavour of the popcorn complements most whiskies, and the bitter chocolate stops the sugar from dominating. Use chocolate with the highest possible proportion of cocoa solids (at least 70%) for the best flavour.

INGREDIENTS
- 1⅓ servings popped popcorn
- 120 g (4 oz) butter, plus extra for forming balls
- 85 g (3 oz) brown sugar
- 120 ml (4 fl oz) whisky
- 1 teaspoon salt
- About 50 g (1¾ oz) plain chocolate, melted, for drizzling (see page 9)

METHOD
Line two large baking trays with nonstick baking paper.

Place the popcorn in a large bowl.

In a medium pan, over a gentle heat, melt the 120 g (4 oz) butter. Add the brown sugar, whisky and salt, stirring frequently until the sugar has dissolved. Increase the heat to medium-high and bring to a boil. Boil for 2 minutes, pour mixture over the popcorn, and toss gently until evenly coated. Let popcorn cool slightly, until cool enough to handle, butter your hands, and form into 10 balls. Place balls on the prepared baking trays. When completely cooled, drizzle with melted plain chocolate. Serve immediately, or store for up to 3 days.

Makes 10 balls.

DATE AND WALNUT POPCORN BARS

The caramel chocolate chips used in this recipe blend beautifully with the flavour of dates and walnuts. For a fabulous dessert, try serving the squares with ice cream and caramel or butterscotch topping.

INGREDIENTS

- 120 g (4 oz) butter,
  plus extra for greasing
- 1 serving popped popcorn
- 120 g (4 oz) coarsely chopped walnuts
- 200 g (7 oz) finely chopped pitted dates
- 300 g (10½ oz) miniature marshmallows
- 175 g (6 oz) caramel milk chocolate
  flavoured drops

METHOD

Lightly grease a 23 x 33-cm (9 x 13-in) baking tray with a little butter.

In a large bowl, place the popcorn, walnuts and dates, and stir to combine. In a large pan, over a gentle heat, melt the remaining butter, marshmallows and caramel milk chocolate flavoured drops, stirring continuously, until smooth. Pour mixture over the popcorn and stir gently to coat evenly. Transfer the popcorn to the baking tray, press into the edges, and smooth the top. Allow to cool before cutting into 24 bars. Store for up to 4 days.

Makes 24 bars.

TIP

Instead of caramel you could use half peanut butter chips and half plain chocolate chips – a delicious, classic combination!

Chapter 3
MAIN DISHES AND DESSERTS

Popcorn is surprisingly versatile when it comes to main dishes.
It can be ground into a powder to use in cornbread or in stuffed
mushrooms; layered like nachos; sizzled with prawns; or made into
tortillas. And for desserts, you can use popcorn in cookies or to
decorate cupcakes and ice cream.

POPCORN MEATLOAF

Replacing breadcrumbs with popcorn is a great way to keep your meatloaf gluten-free. Good-quality beef bouillon and fresh herbs round out the flavour, and served with roast potatoes, green vegetables and your favourite gravy, there will be clean plates all around.

INGREDIENTS
- A little butter for greasing
- ⅔ serving popped popcorn
- 560 g (1 lb 4 oz) extra-lean beef mince
- 1 medium onion, finely chopped
- 2 tablespoons full-fat milk
- 1 egg, lightly beaten
- 3 tablespoons freshly chopped parsley
- 1 tablespoon fresh thyme leaves
- 2 teaspoons good-quality beef stock concentrate
- 2 teaspoons soy sauce
- 2 teaspoons Worcestershire sauce
- 1 clove garlic, finely chopped or crushed
- 1 teaspoon salt
- Freshly ground black pepper, to taste
- 50 ml (2 fl oz) tomato ketchup

METHOD
Preheat the oven to 180° C (350° F, gas mark 4). Lightly grease a 20 x 10-cm (8 x 4-in) loaf tin with butter.

Place the popcorn in a blender or food processor and process until finely ground. Pour into a large bowl. Add the beef mince, onion, milk, egg, parsley, thyme, beef stock concentrate, soy sauce, Worcestershire sauce, garlic, salt and black pepper. Mix with a wooden spoon or your hands until well blended. Press the mixture into the loaf tin and spread the ketchup on top. Bake in the oven, uncovered, for 1 hour or until cooked through. Remove from the oven and allow to cool for 10 minutes before slicing. Serve immediately.

Serves 4.

MUSHROOM AND POPCORN FISH

Choose a fish with firm white flesh, such as snapper, haddock or cod. These are delicious served this way, topped with ground popcorn mixed with dried mushrooms and herbs. Add a little cayenne pepper if you like it hot.

INGREDIENTS

- ½ serving popped popcorn
- 25 g (1 oz) dried porcini or shitake mushrooms
- 2 teaspoons dried oregano
- 2 teaspoons dried basil
- 1 teaspoon garlic powder
- 1 teaspoon onion powder
- 1½ teaspoons salt
- 1 teaspoon ground cumin
- ½ teaspoon cayenne pepper (optional)
- 1 egg, lightly beaten
- 1 to 2 tablespoons vegetable oil
- 4 fish fillets

METHOD

Preheat the oven to 140° C (275° F, gas mark 1).

Place the popcorn, dried mushrooms, oregano, basil, garlic powder, onion powder, salt, ground cumin and cayenne pepper (if using) in a blender or food processor. Process until mixture resembles fine breadcrumbs. Pour into a wide, shallow bowl. Put the beaten egg into another wide, shallow bowl.

Heat the vegetable oil in a large frying pan over medium to high heat. Dip the fish into the egg, coating both sides, and then into the popcorn and mushroom mixture, coating both sides. When the oil is hot, but not smoking, cook the fish for about 3 minutes on each side, or until golden brown and just cooked through. Keep warm in the oven while you cook all the fillets, then serve immediately.

Serves 4.

TIP

To bake this fish in the oven, lightly spray a baking tray with oil, lay the fish fillets on the oiled surface, spray again, and bake at 190° C (375° F, gas mark 5) for 15 minutes.

POPCORN-CRUSTED CHICKEN STRIPS

Instead of frying chicken in breadcrumbs, try coating it with ground popcorn, flavoured with eleven different herbs and spices. Not only is it tasty, it is also gluten-free. If you want to keep the whole dish gluten-free, use rice flour instead of plain flour. Serve with coleslaw or potato salad for a classic all-American meal.

INGREDIENTS

- ½ serving popped popcorn
- 2 teaspoons paprika
- 1 teaspoon dried thyme
- 1 teaspoon dried oregano
- 1 teaspoon dried marjoram
- 1 teaspoon ground ginger
- 1 teaspoon ground sage
- 1 teaspoon celery salt
- 1 teaspoon garlic powder
- ½ teaspoon crushed dried chilli flakes
- 1 teaspoon freshly ground black pepper
- ½ teaspoon salt
- 50 g (1¾ oz) plain flour (or rice flour)
- 1 large egg, beaten
- 450 g (1 lb) skinned chicken breast fillets
- 3 tablespoons vegetable oil
- 1 tablespoon butter

METHOD

Preheat the oven to 140° C (275° F, gas mark 1).

In a food processor, place the popcorn, paprika, thyme, oregano, marjoram, ginger, sage, celery salt, garlic powder, dried chilli flakes, black pepper and salt. Pulse until the mixture resembles coarse breadcrumbs. Transfer to a wide, shallow bowl. Place the flour in another wide, shallow bowl, and the beaten egg in a third bowl.

Cut the chicken into 1.25-cm (½-in) strips and dry with paper towels. Dip each chicken strip first in the flour, coating each side, then in the egg, coating each side, and finally in the popcorn, coating all over.

In a large frying pan, heat the oil and butter together over medium-high heat. When it is hot, but not smoking, add the chicken strips and cook until they are golden brown and cooked through, turning them once while cooking. Do not overcrowd the frying pan; work in batches if necessary, adding a little more oil if needed. Keep the first strips warm in the oven while you cook the rest of the chicken. Serve immediately.

Serves 4.

SIZZLING PRAWN POPCORN

This is a wonderful dish to serve to friends, as an appetiser or as part of a buffet lunch or dinner. It is a spiced seafood cocktail, rich with butter, garlic, mint and parsley, and tossed with prawns and cheese.

INGREDIENTS

- 1 tablespoon unsalted butter
- 50 g (1¾ oz) unpopped popcorn
- 2 teaspoons smoked paprika
- 1 teaspoon dried thyme
- 1 teaspoon ground cumin
- 1 teaspoon dried chilli flakes
- ½ teaspoon salt
- 1 teaspoon freshly ground black pepper
- 4 tablespoons salted butter
- 3 cloves garlic, finely chopped or crushed
- 285 g (10 oz) small cooked prawns
- 40g (1½ oz) roughly chopped flat-leaf parsley
- 25 g (1 oz) roughly chopped mint
- 2 jalapeños, finely sliced
- 1 cup finely grated mature cheddar cheese

METHOD

Place 1 tablespoon unsalted butter with the popcorn kernels in a large pan with a lid. Heat over high heat, lid on, for about 4 minutes, shaking the pan often, until the popping slows down to 2 to 3 pops every few seconds. Remove from the heat and leave for 2 minutes until the popping has stopped. Transfer the popcorn to a large bowl and add the paprika, thyme, ground cumin, dried chilli flakes, salt and black pepper. Stir to combine.

In a large frying pan, melt the salted butter over medium-low heat, add the garlic, and sauté for 2 minutes, stirring continuously. Do not burn, or the garlic will be bitter. Add the prawns and sauté for about 30 seconds only, stirring continuously, and pour over the popcorn in the bowl. Add the parsley, mint, jalapeños, and cheese. Stir gently to combine. Transfer to a serving bowl and serve immediately as part of a buffet, or divide the popcorn mix into small bowls and serve individually.

Serves 6.

POPCORN SALAD

*Toss together just before serving to avoid the popcorn becoming
too soft, and serve as an alternative to coleslaw at a barbecue or buffet.*

INGREDIENTS

- 2 servings popped popcorn
- 12 rashers of bacon
- 250 g (9 oz) finely chopped celery
- 225 g (8 oz) finely grated mature cheddar cheese
- 225 g (8 oz) well-drained finely sliced water chestnuts
- 125 g (4¼ oz) finely sliced spring onions
- 1 red pepper, seeded and finely chopped
- 1 teaspoon salt
- 1 teaspoon freshly ground black pepper
- 250 ml (9 fl oz) mayonnaise

METHOD

Place the popcorn in a large bowl.

In a frying pan over medium-high heat, cook the bacon, in batches if necessary, until it is crisp. Drain on paper towels, crumble, and set aside until cooled.

In another bowl, mix together the celery, cheese (reserving some for topping), water chestnuts, spring onions, red pepper, salt, black pepper and mayonnaise. Stir to combine. Add to the popcorn, stir gently until well combined, sprinkle the remaining cheese on top, and serve immediately.

Serves 10 to 12.

POPCORN NACHOS

Popcorn is layered with jalapeños, tomatoes, cheese and coriander, just like traditional nachos. Top with sour cream and guacamole, just before serving, to make it extra-special. Set it in the centre of the table, give everyone a fork, and tell them to dig in.

INGREDIENTS

- 2 tablespoons butter, plus a little more for greasing
- 2 servings popped popcorn
- 1 to 2 teaspoons chilli powder
- 60g (2 oz) well-drained black olives
- 1 tablespoon coarsely chopped jalapeños
- 2 tablespoons fresh tomatoes, seeded and chopped
- 175 g (6 oz) finely grated mature cheddar cheese
- 50 g (1¾ oz) coarsely chopped coriander
- Sour cream and guacamole (optional)

METHOD

Preheat the oven to 140° C (275° F, gas mark 1). Lightly grease two large cookie trays with a little butter.

Place the popcorn in a large bowl. In a small pan, over a gentle heat, melt the remaining butter and pour it over the popcorn. Sprinkle with the chilli powder and toss to combine.

Place a third of the popcorn on the baking trays, dividing it equally between the two sheets. Layer in turn a third each of the olives, jalapeños, tomatoes and cheese onto the popcorn on each sheet. Repeat the layers twice more until all the ingredients have been used.

Bake in the oven for 10 minutes, until the cheese has melted. Sprinkle with coriander, and serve immediately, accompanied by sour cream and guacamole, if desired.

Serves 8.

TIP

For guacamole, mash together the flesh of 3 avocados, 1 tomato, the juice of 1 lime, 1 small finely chopped red onion, 1 seeded, chopped red chilli and a bunch of coriander.

SPICY MEXICAN POPCORN BREAD

This colourful spicy popcorn bread is a variation of cornbread, where the flour is replaced with popped and ground popcorn kernels, providing a kind of early American pioneer authenticity. You can make it as mild or spicy as you like by adjusting the amount of chillies.

INGREDIENTS
- A little butter for greasing
- ½ serving popped popcorn
- 250 g (9 oz) yellow cornmeal or polenta
- 2 teaspoons salt
- 2 teaspoons freshly ground black pepper
- 1 teaspoon baking powder
- 1 teaspoon bicarbonate of soda
- 40 g (1½ oz) finely chopped spring onions, green part only
- 120 g (4 oz) finely grated cheddar cheese
- 1 or 2 red chilli peppers, mild or hot, finely chopped
- 2 eggs
- 350 ml (12 fl oz) buttermilk
- 1 400-g (14-oz) can creamed corn
- 60 ml (2 fl oz) olive oil

METHOD
Preheat the oven to 190° C (375° F, gas mark 5). Lightly grease a 23 x 33-cm (9 x 13-in) baking tray with butter.

Place the popped corn in a blender or food processor, and process until finely ground. In a large bowl, mix the ground popcorn with the cornmeal or polenta, salt, black pepper, baking powder, bicarbonate of soda, spring onions, cheese and chillies.

In another bowl, whisk the eggs with the buttermilk, creamed corn and olive oil. Make a well in the centre of the popcorn mix and quickly pour in the egg and buttermilk mixture. Stir lightly until just combined, and pour into the prepared pan.

Bake in the oven for 35 to 40 minutes, or until golden brown and cooked through. Cool in the pan for 10 minutes, then turn out to cool on a wire rack.

Cut into squares to serve.

Makes 1 loaf.

POPCORN TORTILLAS

Making your own tortillas is much easier with a tortilla press, but it can be done simply by rolling the dough between two sheets of cling film. Making tortillas is worthwhile because the end result is far superior to shop-bought.

INGREDIENTS

- 35 g (1¼ oz) popped popcorn
- 275 g (9¾ oz) cornflour (more if required)
- ½ teaspoon salt
- 1 tablespoon vegetable oil

METHOD

Place the popcorn in a blender or food processor, and process until finely ground. In a large bowl, mix all the ingredients together to make a stiff dough with 240 ml (8 fl oz) water. You may find it easier to start with a little less water and add more if you need it. If you mix the dough with your hands, it is easier to get a feeling for how dry or sticky it is. If the dough seems too dry, add a little more water. If the mixture is too sticky or wet, add extra cornflour. Unlike pastry, the dough will not suffer from too much handling.

Pinch off a piece of dough the size of a golf ball and roll it into a smooth ball. If you do not have a tortilla press, roll it into a 15-cm (6-in) circle between two sheets of cling film. If you do have a press, set the dough on a piece of plastic in the tortilla press, cover with another piece of cling film, and press.

Transfer the tortilla to a hot, dry frying pan. Cook for 30 to 40 seconds on one side, gently turn, and cook for about 60 seconds. It should puff slightly. Turn back to the first side and cook for another 30 to 40 seconds. Remove and keep warm while you cook the others. Use as you wish.

Makes about 10 tortillas.

TIP

To add extra flavour to your tortillas, add 3 tablespoons coriander or basil, or alternatively add crushed garlic, or finely ground black pepper or flaxseeds.

STUFFED MUSHROOMS

With shallots sautéed in butter, with aromatic parsley and tangy blue cheese, these are a delicious snack or appetiser. Using ground popcorn in the mushroom stuffing instead of breadcrumbs is a welcome change and also means that the dish is gluten-free.

INGREDIENTS

- 1/10 serving popped popcorn
- 4 tablespoons butter
- 4 large flat portobello mushrooms
- 2 shallots, finely chopped
- 175 g (6 oz) crumbled blue cheese
- 50 g (1¾ oz) freshly chopped parsley
- Salt
- Freshly ground black pepper

METHOD

Place the popcorn in a blender or food processor and process until finely ground.

Preheat the oven to 170° C (325° F, gas mark 3). Grease 4 individual ovenproof serving dishes with half the butter. Carefully remove the stems from the mushrooms and chop finely. Wipe the caps with damp paper towels and set aside.

In a small pan, over a gentle heat, melt the remaining butter and add the chopped mushroom stems and shallots. Increase the heat slightly and sauté until the mushrooms and shallots are softened. Remove from the heat and allow to cool for 5 minutes. Add the cheese, parsley and ground popcorn, and season to taste with salt and black pepper. Divide the mixture between the mushroom caps.

Transfer the stuffed mushrooms to the serving dishes. Bake in the oven for about 20 minutes, until golden brown, and serve immediately.

Serves 4.

POPCORN MACAROONS

*Macaroons make a very sophisticated dessert or a beautiful gift. These use
my favourite caramel popcorn and are absolutely scrumptious.*

INGREDIENTS

- 3 egg whites
- 120 g (4 oz) ground almonds
- 250 g (9 oz) icing sugar
- 20 g (¾ oz) Best-Ever Caramel
  and Pecan Popcorn (page 102)
- 2 tablespoons caster sugar
- ½ teaspoon cream of tartar

For the chocolate filling:
- 200 g (7 oz) plain chocolate, chopped
- 170 ml (6 fl oz) plus 2 tablespoons
  double cream
- 1 teaspoon brandy (optional)
- 1 tablespoon butter

METHOD

If possible, 3 days before making these macaroons, separate the egg whites
from the yolks, and store the whites in the refrigerator, covered with a paper
towel. Before baking, let the whites come to room temperature.

Line 2 large baking trays with nonstick baking paper. You can draw
20 5-cm (2-in) circles on the paper if you want, which would make it easier
to pipe the macaroons into equal sizes.

Blend the ground almonds and icing sugar in a food processor until well
combined. Transfer to a small bowl and set aside. In the food processor,
pulse the caramel popcorn into small pieces, transfer to a small bowl, and
set aside.

In a large bowl, using an electric mixer, slowly whisk the egg whites at low
speed until stiff peaks form when the whisk is removed. Slowly whisk in
the caster sugar and cream of tartar until the mixture is smooth and glossy,
increasing the speed of the mixer as the egg whites stiffen. Gently fold in
the blended almonds and sugar until the mixture resembles shaving foam.
Spoon the mixture into a piping bag fitted with a 1.25-cm (½-in) round
nozzle, and pipe 5-cm (2-in) circles onto the nonstick baking paper. If a peak
forms, wet your finger and smooth it down. Sharply tap the bottom of the
pan to release any air bubbles from the macaroons. Sprinkle the popcorn on
top of half of the macaroons, then set them aside for 60 minutes, until no
longer sticky. While the macaroons are drying, preheat the oven to 170° C
(325° F, gas mark 3). Bake the macaroons in the oven for 10 to 15 minutes,
or until cooked through; their outsides should be golden and slightly crisp.
Remove from the oven and allow to cool for 5 minutes. Carefully peel away
the nonstick baking paper and set aside to cool completely.

For the chocolate filling, heat the double cream and chocolate in a medium
pan over a gentle heat, stirring occasionally, until smooth and well
combined. Add the brandy, if using, and the butter, and stir until smooth.
Remove from the heat and allow to cool completely. Use the filling to
sandwich the macaroons together, using the macaroons without popcorn for
the base and the rest for the tops. Chill in the refrigerator for 30 minutes.

Makes about 10 macaroon sandwiches.

CARAMEL POPCORN CUPCAKES

These cupcakes rise beautifully, and are topped with a delicious caramel frosting then decorated with caramel popcorn, adding a sweet and pleasant crunch.

INGREDIENTS

- 120 g (4 oz) butter, plus extra for greasing
- ⅕ servings popped popcorn
- 275 g (9¾ oz) plain flour
- 175 g (6 oz) light brown sugar
- 1 tablespoon baking powder
- 2 large eggs
- 280 ml (9½ fl oz) sour cream
- 1 teaspoon vanilla extract

For the caramel icing:

- 200 g (7 oz) granulated sugar
- 160 g (5½ oz) butter, very soft
- 140 g (5 oz) icing sugar
- 85 g (3 oz) Best-Ever Caramel and Pecan Popcorn (page 102), to serve

METHOD

Preheat the oven to 200° C (400° F, gas mark 6). Line a 12-cup muffin tray with 12 paper or foil muffin cases, and grease a baking sheet with a little butter.

In a small pan, over a gentle heat, melt the remaining butter, then set it aside to cool. Place the popcorn in a blender or food processor, and process until finely ground.

In a medium bowl, mix together the flour, ground popcorn, brown sugar and baking powder. In another medium bowl, beat the eggs and stir in the sour cream, vanilla extract and cooled melted butter. Pour mixture into the dry ingredients. Stir gently until just mixed. Do not overmix; it doesn't matter if there are a few dry bits. Divide the mixture between the muffin cases and bake in the oven for about 25 minutes. Remove, allow to cool in the pan for 5 minutes, then remove from the pan and allow to cool completely on a wire rack.

To make the caramel for the frosting, tip the granulated sugar into a large frying pan, shaking it so it forms an even layer. Heat gently until it melts, tipping the pan to make sure the edges don't burn. Once the sugar is melted to a golden caramel, pour it onto the baking sheet on a heatproof counter. Allow to cool, then crush into small pieces.

To make the frosting, beat the butter and icing sugar together, using an electric mixer. Stir in the crushed caramel bits. Just before serving, pipe or swirl frosting onto the cooled cupcakes and top with caramel popcorn.

Makes 12 cupcakes.

BLUEBERRY AND WHITE CHOCOLATE POPCORN MUFFINS

The sweetness of white chocolate is offset by fresh blueberries in these muffins, which are made with ground popcorn and buttermilk. If you wish, you could use plain chocolate chips rather than white chocolate.

INGREDIENTS

- ⅕ serving popped popcorn
- 175 g (6 oz) plain flour
- 4 teaspoons baking powder
- A pinch of salt
- 100 g (3½ oz) sugar
- 175 g (6 oz) white chocolate chips
- 110 g (3¾ oz) fresh blueberries
- 2 large eggs
- 6 tablespoons vegetable oil
- 250 ml (9 fl oz) buttermilk
- 1 teaspoon vanilla extract

METHOD

Place the popcorn in a blender or food processor and process until finely ground.

Preheat the oven to 200° C (400° F, gas mark 6). Line a 12-cup muffin tray with paper muffin cases. In a bowl, sift together the flour, baking powder and salt. Stir in the ground popcorn, sugar, white chocolate chips and blueberries. In another bowl, whisk the eggs, then whisk in the oil, buttermilk and vanilla extract.

Make a well in the centre of the dry ingredients and quickly pour in the wet ingredients. Stir quickly and lightly until just combined. It does not matter if there are a few lumps and dry bits. Spoon quickly into the muffin cups and bake for 20 to 25 minutes until golden, firm to the touch, and well risen. Leave in the pan for 5 minutes, then transfer to a wire rack to cool. Serve warm or allow to cool completely.

Makes 12 muffins.

TIP

Try omitting the blueberries, changing the chocolate chips to plain, and adding 60 g (2 oz) chopped pecans. Alternatively you could swap the blueberries for chopped, hulled strawberries.

BUTTERSCOTCH POPCORN BROWNIES

Instead of chocolate brownies, why not try rich and luscious melt-in-the-mouth butterscotch-flavoured brownies instead, with the added texture of popcorn blended in the mix?

INGREDIENTS
- A little butter for greasing
- ⅓ serving popped popcorn
- 175 g (6 oz) dark brown sugar
- 60 ml (2 fl oz) vegetable oil
- 1 egg
- 120 g (4 oz) coarsely chopped pecans
- 100g (3½ oz) caramel milk chocolate flavoured drops
- 1 teaspoon vanilla extract
- 50 g (1¾ oz) plain flour
- 1 teaspoon baking powder
- ½ teaspoon salt

METHOD
Preheat oven to 180° C (350° F, gas mark 4). Lightly grease a 20 x 20-cm (8 x 8-in) square baking tray with butter. Line the base with nonstick baking paper.

Place the popcorn in a blender or food processor and process until coarsely ground.

In a large bowl, stir together brown sugar, oil and egg until smooth. Mix in pecans, caramel milk chocolate chips and vanilla extract. In a medium bowl, mix together ground popcorn, plain flour, baking powder and salt. Add to the brown sugar and egg mixture, stirring well. Spread batter evenly in the buttered pan. Bake for 20 minutes, remove from the oven, and allow to cool. Cut into 9 squares while still warm.

Makes 9 brownies.

TIP
Chocolate and peanut butter work really well together in brownies. Substitute peanut butter chips for caramel, and add 50 g (1¾ oz) plain chocolate chips and 1 tablespoon cocoa powder with the flour.

FRUITY POPCORN COOKIES

These tasty cookies are packed full of goodness. With coconut and raisins, wheat germ and oats, they are a great energy-giving snack for the children after school. Kids will love the idea of putting popcorn in cookies.

INGREDIENTS

- 120 g (4 oz) butter, softened, plus extra for greasing
- 50 g (1¾ oz) plain flour
- 2 teaspoons baking powder
- ½ teaspoon bicarbonate of soda
- ½ teaspoon salt
- 175 g (6 oz) light brown sugar
- 1 large egg, beaten
- 1 teaspoon vanilla extract
- 140 g (5 oz) toasted wheat germ
- 40 g (1½ oz) rolled oats
- 40 g (1½ oz) sweetened coconut flakes
- ½ serving popped popcorn
- 175 g (6 oz) raisins
- 60 g (2 oz) coarsely chopped pecans

METHOD

Preheat the oven to 180° C (350° F, gas mark 4). Lightly grease two large cookie trays with a little butter.

In a small bowl, sift together the flour, baking powder, bicarbonate of soda and salt. Set aside. In another medium bowl, mix the remaining butter and brown sugar together briskly with a wooden spoon, then add the egg a little at a time, mixing briskly after each addition. Stir in the vanilla extract. Lightly fold in the flour mix with the wheat germ, oats, coconut, popcorn, raisins and pecans. Mix until just blended. Drop rounded teaspoons onto the baking trays, allowing 5 cm (2 in) between the cookies for spreading.

Bake in the oven for 7 to 8 minutes, or until the edges of the cookies are lightly browned. Remove from the oven and allow to cool on the baking trays for 5 minutes before transferring to wire racks to cool completely.

Makes about 45 cookies.

CARAMEL CORN AND PECAN ICE CREAM

This is a rich and creamy vanilla ice cream, full of clumps of my Best-Ever Caramel and Pecan Popcorn (page 102). Don't try to use a different caramel corn – my recipe stays much crispier, even in a dessert, because the popcorn is surrounded by a hard coating of crispy caramel. Serve this ice cream with a caramel sauce and extra caramel popcorn, if desired.

INGREDIENTS

- 4 egg yolks
- 135 g (4½ oz) sugar
- 140 ml (4¾ fl oz) full-fat milk
- 140 ml (4¾ fl oz) single cream
- 280 ml (9½ fl oz) double cream
- 1 teaspoon vanilla extract
- ¼ serving Best-Ever Caramel and Pecan Popcorn (page 102)
- Extra caramel and pecan popcorn and caramel sauce, to serve (optional)

METHOD

In a large bowl, beat the egg yolks and sugar together until creamy. In a medium pan over medium heat, bring the milk and single cream just to a boil, pour it onto the egg yolks, and mix thoroughly. Transfer to the top of a double boiler (or set a heatproof bowl over a pan of hot water) and cook, stirring continuously, until the mixture is thick enough to coat the back of a spoon. Strain into a medium bowl and set aside until cool.

In a large bowl, whip the double cream until it stands in soft peaks. Fold the cooled egg yolk mixture into the whipped cream with the vanilla extract, and pour the mixture into a rigid freezer container. Cover and freeze for about 2 hours, or until ice crystals have formed around the edges and it is partly frozen. Remove from the freezer, whisk well, and fold in the Caramel and Pecan Popcorn. Return to the freezer until firm.

Transfer to the refrigerator about 45 minutes before serving to soften.

To serve, scoop into chilled glasses and add extra caramel popcorn and caramel sauce, if desired.

Serves 4.

POPCORN PARTY CAKE

This is a quick and easy party cake to make with popcorn. You can change the colours depending upon the time of year. It is gooey and chewy, and sure to be a hit.

INGREDIENTS

- 4 tablespoons butter, cut into cubes, plus extra for greasing
- 450 g (1 lb) miniature marshmallows
- 20 toffees, unwrapped
- 1⅓ servings popped popcorn
- 135 g (4½ oz) Spanish peanuts
- 35 g (1¼ oz) coarsely broken pretzels
- 200 g (7 oz) chocolate M&Ms, colour as desired

METHOD

Grease a 25-cm (10-in) round cake tin liberally with butter.

In a large pan, over a gentle heat, melt the 4 tablespoons butter, marshmallows and caramels together, stirring occasionally. Place the popcorn, peanuts, pretzels and M&Ms in a large bowl. Pour the melted marshmallow mixture over the popcorn mixture, and mix well. Press into the cake tin, smooth the top, and set aside to cool at room temperature, until firm. Remove from tin and cut with a serrated knife.

Serves about 12.

POPCORN GÂTEAU GANACHE

Your friends and family will be impressed by this dessert. Crispy meringue filled with chocolate-flavoured cream, topped with caramel popcorn and drizzled with chocolate.

INGREDIENTS

- A little butter for greasing
- 135 g (4½oz) hazelnuts
- 4 large egg whites, at room temperature
- 200 g (7 oz) sugar
- 1 teaspoon vanilla extract
- 1 teaspoon malt vinegar
- 280 ml (9½ fl oz) double cream

For the chocolate sauce:
- 175 g (6 oz) plain chocolate
- 250 g (9 oz) sugar
- 1 recipe Best-Ever Caramel and Pecan Popcorn (see page 102)

METHOD

Preheat the oven to 180° C (350° F, gas mark 4). Lightly grease two 20-cm (8-in) round cake tins with a little butter, and line each one with nonstick baking paper.

In a dry medium frying pan, toast the hazelnuts until they are light golden. Remove from the heat and set aside until cool. Place them in a blender and process until they are finely ground. Set aside.

In a large, squeaky clean bowl, whisk the egg whites until stiff, then gradually whisk in 200 g (7 oz) sugar, a tablespoon or so at a time. Keep whisking until the meringue is very stiff. Carefully fold in the vanilla, vinegar and ground hazelnuts. Divide the mixture between the tins and bake in the oven for 45 to 50 minutes. Cool on a wire rack.

To make the chocolate sauce, in a small pan, over a gentle heat, heat the chocolate, sugar and 150 ml (5 fl oz) water until the sugar has dissolved. Increase the heat to medium, and simmer for 10 minutes, stirring occasionally. Remove from the heat and set aside to cool.

Place the double cream in a medium bowl, add 4 tablespoons of the chocolate sauce, and whip until it stands in soft peaks. Pour the remainder of the chocolate sauce into a small serving jug, and set aside. Sandwich the meringue rounds together with three-quarters of the chocolate cream, and pipe the remaining cream all around the edge. Arrange the caramel popcorn on top, filling all the space. Put the melted chocolate in a nonstick baking paper piping bag (see page 9), snip off the end, and drizzle the chocolate over the popcorn in lines. Serve immediately, and pass around the chocolate sauce separately.

Serves 6.

TIP

A delicious variation is to serve a melba sauce instead of chocolate. Rub 225 g (8 oz) raspberries through a sieve into a bowl, beat in 4 tablespoons icing sugar, and serve on the side.

Chapter 4
CHOCOLATE AND SWEETS

For those of us with a sweet tooth, this is the ultimate treat. Popcorn wrapped
in caramel, or smothered in chocolate and mixed with nuts, or packed with
fruit – this chapter is full of endless possibilities. Have fun turning popcorn
into the perfect sweet treat for all ages, from Candy Cane Popcorn for the kids
to Limoncello Popcorn for your adult friends.

PUPPY CHOW

*This is a quick and easy snack to make. It is sweet and tasty,
full of chocolate and peanut butter, and children will love it.*

INGREDIENTS

- 2 servings popped popcorn
- 275 g (9¾ oz) plain chocolate chips
- 200 g (7 oz) smooth peanut putter
- 75 g (2¾ oz) unsalted butter
- 1 teaspoon vanilla extract
- 275 g (9¾ oz) icing sugar

METHOD

Put the popcorn in a large bowl. Place the chocolate chips,
peanut butter and butter in a heatproof bowl set over a pan of
barely simmering water to melt. Stir until smooth, add the vanilla,
and stir to combine.

Pour the chocolate mixture over the popcorn and stir gently until
the popcorn is evenly coated. Sift the icing sugar over the chocolate-
covered popcorn, and stir until each piece is evenly coated with sugar.
Spread out the mixture on a large baking sheet and set aside for about
20 minutes, or until the chocolate is set. Break it up in manageable
pieces and serve immediately, or store for up to 3 days.

Makes 2 medium servings.

HONEY NUT POPCORN

The sweetness of the honey blends beautifully with the almonds and apricots,
and the hint of cinnamon lifts the flavour out of the ordinary.

INGREDIENTS

- 120 g (4 oz) butter,
  plus extra for greasing
- 2 servings popped popcorn
- 1 teaspoon salt, or to taste
- 120 g (4 oz) finely chopped almonds
- 50 g (1¾ oz) finely chopped dried apricots
- 5 tablespoons honey
- 1 teaspoon ground cinnamon

METHOD

Preheat the oven to 180° C (350° F, gas mark 4). Lightly grease 2 large baking sheets with a little butter.

In a large bowl, place the popcorn, salt, almonds and apricots, and stir to combine. In a small pan, over a gentle heat, melt the remaining butter and honey. Add the cinnamon, then pour mixture over the popcorn, almonds and apricots. Stir gently to combine, then transfer to the baking sheets. Bake in the oven for 15 minutes, remove, and leave to cool. Either serve immediately or store for up to 4 days.

Makes 2 medium servings.

TIP

If you are intolerant to dairy products, it's fine to substitute dairy-free margarine for the butter, both in the recipe and to grease the baking trays.

GINGERBREAD POPCORN

This is caramel popcorn with lots of ginger, nutmeg and cinnamon, which give the popcorn a delightful gingerbread flavour and a wonderful aroma.

INGREDIENTS
- 225 g (8 oz) butter, plus extra for greasing
- 2 servings popped popcorn
- 350 g (12 oz) light brown sugar
- 30 ml (1 fl oz) golden syrup
- 30 ml (1 fl oz) treacle
- 90 g (3¼ oz) glucose syrup
- 1 tablespoon ground ginger
- 2 teaspoons ground cinnamon
- ½ teaspoon ground nutmeg
- ½ teaspoon salt
- ½ teaspoon bicarbonate of soda

METHOD
Preheat the oven to 130° C (250° F, gas mark 1/2). Lightly grease a large roasting tin with a little butter. Spread out the popcorn in the roasting tin and set aside.

In a large pan, melt 225 g (8 oz) butter over a gentle heat, then add the brown sugar, golden syrup, treacle, glucose syrup, ginger, cinnamon, nutmeg and salt. Stir until the sugar has dissolved, then increase the heat to medium-high and bring to a boil. Boil for 5 minutes, stirring frequently, and remove from the heat. Add the bicarbonate of soda (the mixture will bubble up), and stir until combined.

Pour mixture over the popcorn, stir gently until evenly coated, and bake in the oven for 1 hour, stirring every 15 minutes, to completely coat the popcorn with the gingerbread caramel. Remove from the oven, stir once more, and allow to cool. Break up any large lumps with your hands after the popcorn has cooled a little. Can be stored for up to 5 days.

Makes about 700 g (1½ lb).

BEST-EVER CARAMEL AND PECAN POPCORN

This popcorn is simply divine. It is baked in the oven and stirred every 10 minutes, which coats every popcorn kernel with sweet, crunchy, and delicious caramel.

INGREDIENTS

- 120 g (4 oz) butter, plus extra for greasing
- 2 servings popped popcorn
- 120 g (4 oz) pecan halves
- 1 teaspoon salt
- 175 g (6 oz) light brown sugar
- 175 g (6 oz) glucose syrup
- ¼ teaspoon bicarbonate of soda

METHOD

Preheat the oven to 130° C (250° F, gas mark 1/2). Lightly grease a large roasting tray with a little butter.

Spread the popcorn and pecans on the roasting tray, sprinkle with salt, and set aside. In a medium pan, over a gentle heat, melt the remaining butter, brown sugar, glucose syrup and bicarbonate of soda together. Increase the heat to medium and bring to a boil. Cook, without stirring, until the mixture reaches 112° C (235° F) on a sugar thermometer, about 7 minutes. Remove from the heat and carefully pour the hot caramel over the popcorn and pecans. Stir the mixture with a wooden spoon to evenly coat all the popcorn and nuts.

Bake in the oven for 1 hour, gently stirring the popcorn and pecans every 10 minutes to completely coat them with caramel. Be careful not to break the popcorn pieces while stirring. Remove from the oven, stir once more, and set aside to cool. If there are any large clumps, break them apart carefully with your fingers when the popcorn has cooled a little. Can be stored for up to 5 days.

Makes 2 large servings.

TIP

Do not be tempted to leave the popcorn to its own devices in the oven for longer than 10 minutes: regular stirring is the secret to success in this recipe.

CANDY CANE POPCORN

Crushed candy canes are mixed with popcorn and white chocolate, making a sweet and minty popcorn treat for Christmas time (or any time you want!).

INGREDIENTS

- 2 servings popped popcorn
- 10 large candy canes (to give about 300 g (10½ oz) crushed candy canes)
- 400 g (14 oz) white chocolate chips

METHOD

Line 2 large baking trays with nonstick baking paper.

Place the popcorn in a large bowl. Place the candy canes in a food processor and pulse until they are almost completely crushed. Alternatively, place them in a large resealable plastic bag, and use a rolling pin to smash the candy canes until they are finely ground, with just a few larger pieces remaining.

Place the chocolate chips in a heatproof bowl set over a pan of barely simmering water to melt. When they have melted, remove the bowl from the heat and stir until smooth. Add half the crushed candy canes to the white chocolate and stir to combine. Pour the mixture over the popcorn and stir gently until the popcorn is evenly coated.

Spread the popcorn out on the nonstick baking paper to cool. Immediately sprinkle the other half of the crushed candy canes over the top. Set aside until cooled. Break up any large clumps and either serve immediately or store for up to 4 days.

Makes 2 medium servings.

TUTTI-FRUTTI POPCORN

Popcorn cooked with a light caramel is baked with red glacé cherries, pecans, pistachios, cranberries and raisins. What a colourful, sugary treat!

INGREDIENTS

- 175 g (6 oz) butter, plus extra for greasing
- 2 servings popped popcorn
- 100 g (3½ oz) red glacé cherries
- 60 g (2 oz) coarsely chopped pecans
- 40 g (1½ oz) coarsely chopped pistachios
- 50 g (1¾ oz) dried cranberries
- 50 g (1¾ oz) raisins
- 250 g (9 oz) brown sugar
- ½ teaspoon bicarbonate of soda
- 1 teaspoon vanilla extract

METHOD

Preheat the oven to 150° C (300° F, gas mark 2). Lightly grease 2 large baking trays with a little butter.

Place the popcorn in a large bowl and add the red cherries, pecans, pistachios, dried cranberries and raisins. Set aside.

In a large pan, over a gentle heat, melt the remaining butter, add the brown sugar, increase the heat to medium-high, and bring to a boil. Boil for 5 minutes, remove from the heat, and add the bicarbonate of soda and vanilla. Pour mixture over the popcorn, stirring gently until the popcorn is evenly coated.

Spread popcorn on the baking trays and bake in the oven for 30 minutes, stirring twice during the cooking time. Remove from the oven, stir once more, and leave until cooled. Break up any large clumps with your hands when slightly coolec. Can be stored for up to 4 days.

Makes 2 medium servings.

TIP

This popcorn is delicious with a coating of about 100 g (3½ oz) of melted white chocolate. Pour it over the popcorn after it has cooled, and leave until set.

SUPER QUICK CARAMEL POPCORN

This popcorn snack is really fast to prepare. Just melt the caramel chocolate chips with glucose syrup and butter, mix with the popcorn and nuts, and bake in the oven. Job done.

INGREDIENTS

- 75 g (2¾ oz) butter, plus extra for greasing
- 2 servings popped popcorn
- 120 g (4 oz) chopped macadamia nuts
- 350 g (12 oz) caramel milk chocolate flavoured drops
- 450 g (15½ oz) glucose syrup

METHOD

Preheat the oven to 150° C (300° F, gas mark 2). Lightly grease 2 large baking trays with a little butter.

Place the popcorn in a large bowl, add the macadamia nuts, and stir to combine. Set aside.

In a large pan, over a gentle heat, melt the remaining butter, caramel drops and corn syrup together. Increase the heat and bring to a boil. Boil for 5 minutes, then pour over the popcorn. Stir gently to combine. Transfer to the baking trays and bake in the oven for about 45 minutes, stirring every 10 minutes. Remove from the oven, stir once more, and allow to cool. Can be stored for up to 5 days.

Makes 2 medium servings.

PRALINE POPCORN

Brown sugar and maple syrup combine to make this popcorn taste like rich praline.

INGREDIENTS

- 150 g (5½ oz) butter, plus extra for greasing
- 2 servings popped popcorn
- 275 g (9¾ oz) pecan halves
- 175 g (6 oz) brown sugar
- 350 g (12 oz) maple syrup
- 2 teaspoons vanilla extract

METHOD

Preheat the oven to 130° C (250° F, gas mark 1/2). Lightly grease a large roasting tray with a little butter.

Place the popcorn in a large bowl, add the pecans, and stir to combine. In a large pan, heat the remaining butter with the brown sugar and maple syrup over a gentle heat until the sugar has dissolved. Increase the heat to medium-high and bring to a boil. Boil for 5 minutes, remove from the heat, and add the vanilla. Pour over the popcorn and stir gently to combine. Transfer to the roasting tray and bake in the oven for 1 hour, stirring every 10 minutes to ensure the popcorn is evenly coated with caramel. Remove from the oven, stir once more, and allow to cool slightly. Break up any large clumps with your hands and cool completely. Can be stored for up to 1 week.

Makes 2 medium servings.

WHITE CHOCOLATE AND CHERRY POPCORN

White chocolate and cherries are a fantastic combination of flavours.
Throw in some walnuts and the result is perfect.

INGREDIENTS

- 2 servings popped popcorn
- 120 g (4 oz) white chocolate, chopped
- 2 teaspoons butter
- 120 g (4 oz) dried cherries
- 120 g (4 oz) coarsely chopped walnuts
- 1 teaspoon salt

METHOD

Line 2 large baking trays with nonstick baking paper.

Place the popcorn in a large bowl. In a heatproof bowl set over a pan of barely simmering water, melt the white chocolate and butter together. Remove from the heat and stir until smooth. Pour over the popcorn and add the cherries and walnuts. Stir gently until combined. Spread out on the paper-lined baking trays, sprinkle with salt, and set aside to cool before serving. Can be stored for up to 5 days.

Makes 2 medium servings.

HAWAIIAN POPCORN

*The classic Hawaiian flavours of pineapple, macadamia nuts and coconut
are blended into a delicious concoction with popcorn at the centre.*

INGREDIENTS

- 4 tablespoons butter, plus extra
  for greasing
- 2 servings popped popcorn
- 175 g (6 oz) chopped dried apricots
- 75 g (6 oz) chopped candied pineapple
- 85 g (3 oz) sweetened shredded coconut
- 120 g (4 oz) coarsely chopped
  macadamia nuts
- 60 g (2 oz) brown sugar
- 2 tablespoons glucose syrup
- 2 teaspoons vanilla extract

METHOD

Preheat the oven to 150° C (300° F, gas mark 2). Lightly grease two large baking trays with a little butter. Line a large roasting tray with nonstick baking paper.

Place the popcorn in a large bowl. Add the apricots, pineapple, coconut and macadamia nuts, and stir to combine.

In a medium pan, place the remaining butter, brown sugar and glucose syrup, and over a gentle heat, warm until the butter has melted and the sugar has dissolved. Increase the heat to medium-high and bring to a boil. Boil for 2 minutes, remove from the heat, add the vanilla, and stir to combine.

Pour mixture over the popcorn, fruit and nuts, and stir gently until they are evenly coated. Transfer to the baking trays and bake in the oven for about 15 minutes, stirring every 5 minutes. Watch carefully, as the coconut will burn quite easily. Remove from the oven, stir once more, transfer to the paper-lined roasting tray, and allow to cool before serving. Can be stored for up to 5 days.

Makes 2 large servings.

PRALINE COFFEE POPCORN

This popcorn snack is full of pecans and infused with the flavour of coffee, which gives a faint kick of caffeine for extra energy.

INGREDIENTS

- 120 g (4 oz) butter, plus extra for greasing
- 2 servings popped popcorn
- 175 g (6 oz) pecan halves
- 175 g (6 oz) brown sugar
- 3 tablespoons golden syrup
- 3 teaspoons instant coffee granules
- 1 teaspoon vanilla extract

METHOD

Preheat the oven to 140° C (275° F, gas mark 1). Lightly grease 2 large baking trays with a little butter.

Place the popcorn in a large bowl, add the pecans, and stir to combine.

In a large pan, set over a gentle heat, melt 120 g (4 oz) cup butter with the brown sugar, golden syrup and instant coffee. Stir until the sugar has dissolved. Increase the heat to medium-high and bring to a boil. Boil for 2 minutes, remove from the heat, add the vanilla, and stir to combine. Pour over the popcorn and pecans and stir gently until they are evenly coated. Transfer to the baking trays and bake in the oven for about 15 minutes, stirring every 5 minutes. Remove from the oven, stir once more, and allow to cool before serving. Can be stored for up to 1 week.

Makes 2 medium servings.

FRUIT AND NUT POPCORN

This popcorn snack is a quickly prepared, simple and healthy treat. It is not mixed with sugar or baked. It is just tossed together and served straightaway.

INGREDIENTS

- 2 servings popped popcorn
- 250 g (9 oz) golden raisins
- 250 g (9 oz) currants
- 250 g (9 oz) chopped dried apricots
- 135 g (4½ oz) roasted and salted cashews
- 1 teaspoon salt (optional)

METHOD

Place the popcorn in a large bowl. Add the raisins, currants, apricots and cashews. Toss lightly together and sprinkle with a little salt, if desired.

Makes 2 large servings.

TIP

For a more festive variation to this recipe, swap the golden raisins and currants for dried mixed berries, and instead of cashew nuts use chopped roasted and salted mixed nuts.

APPLE PIE POPCORN

Every bit as good as apple pie, this popcorn evokes all those flavours. It is so simple to put together. Great for lunch boxes, and great for any day of the year.

INGREDIENTS

- 4 tablespoons butter, plus extra for greasing
- 2 teaspoons ground cinnamon
- ½ teaspoon ground nutmeg
- 2 tablespoons brown sugar
- ¼ teaspoon vanilla extract
- 150 g (5½ oz) coarsely chopped dried apples
- 1⅓ servings popped popcorn
- 225 g (8 oz) pecan halves

METHOD

Preheat the oven to 150° C (300° F, gas mark 2). Lightly grease a large baking tray with a little butter.

In a small pan, over a gentle heat, melt the remaining butter, and add the cinnamon, nutmeg, brown sugar and vanilla. Remove from the heat. Place the apples, popcorn and pecans on the baking tray, stir to combine, and drizzle the butter mix on the top. Bake in the oven for 20 minutes, stirring after 10 minutes. Remove from the oven, stir once more, and allow to cool before serving. Can be stored for up to 5 days.

Makes 2 small servings.

KAHLÚA, CHERRY AND ALMOND POPCORN

Kahlúa, made from coffee beans and sugarcane, is used in the caramel coating. It adds a special touch with the cherries and almonds, making this popcorn snack truly delectable.

INGREDIENTS

- 2 servings popped popcorn
- 200 g (7 oz) roasted almonds (page 9)
- 85 g (3 oz) dried cherries
- 400g (13¾ oz) sugar
- 240 ml (8 fl oz) Kahlúa
- 450 ml (15 fl oz) white vinegar
- 4 tablespoons cider vinegar
- 6 tablespoons unsalted butter

METHOD

Preheat the oven to 130° C (250° F, gas mark 1/2).

Place the popcorn, almonds and cherries in a large heatproof bowl. Stir to combine, then keep warm in the oven.

In a large pan, heat the sugar, Kahlúa and vinegar over a gentle heat, and stir until the sugar has dissolved. Increase the heat to medium-high and bring mixture to a boil. Add the butter and boil until the temperature on a sugar thermometer reaches 150° C (300° F).

Remove the bowl of popcorn, almonds and cherries from the oven. Pour the butter-sugar mix over the top and stir gently to combine. Allow to cool before serving. Can be stored for up to 1 week.

Makes 2 medium servings.

TIP

If you would prefer not to use alcohol in this recipe, substitute 350 g (12 oz) of glucose syrup and 2 teaspoons instant coffee and add to the pan while the sugar is dissolving.

CINDER TOFFEE POPCORN

This popcorn snack starts with cinder toffee, which, when added to just-out-of-the-oven Best-Ever Caramel and Pecan Popcorn (page 102), adds a distinctive toffee flavour and aerated texture to the divine explosion of sugar on your taste buds.

INGREDIENTS

For the cinder toffee:
- Oil, for greasing baking tray
- 200 g (7 oz) granulated sugar
- 350 g (12 oz) glucose syrup
- 1 teaspoon white wine vinegar
- 1 teaspoon vanilla extract
- 2 teaspoons bicarbonate of soda

- 1 recipe Best-Ever Caramel and Pecan Popcorn (see page 102), omitting the pecans
- 150 g (5½ oz) cup dark chocolate chips

METHOD

First prepare the cinder toffee. You will need a very large saucepan, because when the bicarbonate of soda is added, the toffee will quadruple in size. Have a whisk ready to use. Generously oil a 23 x 33-cm (9 x 13-in) metal baking tray.

In a very large saucepan, over a gentle heat, stir together the sugar, corn syrup, vinegar and vanilla. When the sugar has dissolved, increase the heat to medium-high and bring to a boil. Boil for 3 minutes without stirring, until it is an amber colour. Have the whisk ready, add the bicarbonate of soda, and whisk until fully combined. The mixture will bubble up in the pan. Pour the toffee carefully onto the oiled baking tray and let it set. When cool, break into pieces. The cinder toffee can be stored for up to 2 days in an airtight container.

Prepare the caramel popcorn. Remove it from the oven, give a quick stir, and while it is still hot, sprinkle the cinder toffee and chocolate chips over the top. Set aside to cool before serving. Can be stored for up to 4 days.

Makes 2 medium servings.

CRANBERRY PUNCH POPCORN

*Cranberry juice mixed with sugar syrup adds an enhanced fruity flavour
to cranberries, almonds and popcorn.*

INGREDIENTS

- 120 g (4 oz) butter,
  plus extra for greasing
- 2 servings popped popcorn
- 175 g (6 oz) dried cranberries
- 135 g (4½ oz) whole almonds
- 85 g (3 oz) brown sugar
- 90 g (3¼ oz) glucose syrup
- 2 tablespoons cranberry juice
- 2 teaspoons vanilla extract
- ½ teaspoon bicarbonate of soda

METHOD

Preheat the oven to 140° C (275° F, gas mark 1). Lightly grease
2 large baking trays with a little butter. Place the popcorn
in a large bowl, add the cranberries and almonds, and stir to
combine. Set aside.

In a large pan, over a gentle heat, stir together the 120 g (4 oz)
butter, brown sugar, glucose syrup and cranberry juice. When the
sugar has dissolved, increase the heat to medium-high and bring
to a boil. Boil for 2 minutes, remove from the heat, and stir in the
vanilla and bicarbonate of soda. Be careful, as the mixture will
bubble up.

Pour the syrup over the popcorn, cranberries and almonds, and
stir to evenly coat them. Transfer to the baking trays and bake in
the oven for 30 minutes, stirring every 10 minutes. Remove from
the oven, stir once more, and set aside to cool before serving.
Can be stored for up to 5 days.

Makes 2 medium servings.

PINEAPPLE AND COCONUT POPCORN

The tropical island flavours of pineapple, coconut, banana and cashews blend together to form a wonderful treat for weekend movie watching.

INGREDIENTS

- 4 tablespoons butter, plus extra for greasing
- 2 servings popped popcorn
- 85 g (3 oz) sweetened coconut flakes, lightly toasted (page 9)
- 60 g (2 oz) natural cashews
- 75 g (2¾ oz) chopped candied or dried pineapple
- 85 g (3 oz) dried banana slices
- 90 g (3¼ oz) glucose syrup
- 60 ml (2 fl oz) coconut cream
- 175 g (6 oz) brown sugar

METHOD

Preheat the oven to 150° C (300° F, gas mark 2). Lightly grease 2 large baking trays with a little butter.

Place the popcorn in a large bowl and add the toasted coconut, cashews, pineapple and banana slices. Stir to combine.

In a large pan, over a gentle heat, stir together the remaining butter, glucose syrup, coconut cream and sugar. When the butter has melted and the sugar has dissolved, increase the heat to medium-high and bring to a boil. Boil for 2 minutes, remove from the heat, and pour over the popcorn, fruit and nuts. Stir gently to combine, then transfer to the baking trays. Bake in the oven for 30 minutes, stirring every 10 minutes. Remove from the oven, stir once more, and allow to cool before serving. Can be stored up to 4 days.

Makes 2 large servings.

ALMOND POPCORN CRUNCH

*Almonds and salted peanuts mixed with crunchy pretzels and chocolate
combine to produce a sweet and salty snack that is irresistible.*

INGREDIENTS

- 2 servings popped popcorn
- 175 g (6 oz) broken pretzels
- 135 g (4½ oz) roasted and salted peanuts
- 100 g (3½ oz) flaked almonds
- 550 g (1 lb 4 oz) plain chocolate, chopped

METHOD

Line a large roasting tray with nonstick baking paper.

Place the popcorn, pretzels and peanuts in a large bowl, and stir
to combine. In a large dry frying pan, over medium heat, lightly
toast the almonds until lightly browned, remove from the heat, and
set aside to cool slightly.

In a heatproof bowl set over a pan of barely simmering water,
melt the chocolate and stir until smooth. Stir in the almonds.
Pour chocolate over the popcorn mix. Stir gently to combine,
then spread on the paper-lined roasting tray to set. When cool,
either serve immediately or store for up to 4 days.

Makes 2 large servings.

TIP

Instead of plain pretzels, try using chocolate or vanilla-coated
pretzels instead, or swap the peanuts and almonds for cashew and
macadamia nuts.

RUM RAISIN POPCORN

With plump rum-soaked raisins and a light caramel, this delectable popcorn treat will please the adults in the family.

INGREDIENTS

- 350 g (12 oz) raisins
- 60 ml (2 fl oz) dark rum
- 2 servings popped popcorn
- 3 tablespoons butter, plus extra for greasing
- 175 g (6 oz) brown sugar
- 175 g (6 oz) glucose syrup
- 2 teaspoons rum extract
- 1 teaspoon vanilla extract

METHOD

In a medium bowl, combine the raisins and rum. Set aside to soak for 1 to 2 hours, stirring occasionally. Drain well. Place raisins in a large bowl with the popcorn and set aside.

Lightly grease 2 large baking trays with a little butter.

In a large pan, over a gentle heat, place the remaining butter, brown sugar, and glucose syrup. Stir until the sugar has dissolved. Increase the heat to medium-high and bring to a boil. Boil, without stirring, until the temperature on a sugar thermometer reaches 140° C (280° F). Remove the pan from heat and add the rum extract and vanilla. Pour over the popcorn and raisins, and stir gently to combine. Spread out on the baking trays and set aside to cool completely. Break up any large clumps with your hands before serving. Can be stored for up to 4 days.

Makes 2 medium servings.

GOLD-DUSTED CHOCOLATE HAZELNUT POPCORN

This is a great way to enjoy your popcorn fix. Sparkling with edible gold dust, and spiced with dried chillies, this snack will tick all the boxes, if you like it hot.

INGREDIENTS

- 1½ tablespoons butter, plus extra for greasing
- 120 g (4 oz) chopped hazelnuts
- 2 servings popped popcorn
- 1 teaspoon crushed dried chilli flakes
- ½ teaspoon salt
- 150 g (5¼ oz) dark chocolate, roughly chopped
- 250 ml full-fat milk
- 250 ml single cream
- 175 g (6 oz) chocolate hazelnut spread
- 1 teaspoon edible gold dust

METHOD

Preheat the oven to 180° C (350° F, gas mark 4). Lightly grease a large roasting tray with a little butter. Spread out the hazelnuts in a single layer and roast in the oven for 5 minutes. Remove the pan from the oven and give it a shake, then return it to the oven for another 5 minutes. Keep checking that the nuts are not burning. Remove the pan and turn the oven down to 130° C (250° F, gas mark 1/2). Add the popcorn to the pan with the hazelnuts and stir gently to combine. Sprinkle with crushed dried chilli flakes and salt. Wait 5 minutes until the oven has dropped in temperature, then return the pan to the oven to keep warm.

In a large pan, over a gentle heat, melt together the chocolate, remaining butter, milk and single cream. Stir in the hazelnut spread, and continue stirring until smooth. Remove the warm popcorn and hazelnuts from the oven, and pour the chocolate mixture over the top. Stir gently to combine. Sprinkle with edible gold dust and set aside to cool before serving. Can be stored for up to 4 days.

Makes 2 medium servings.

ORANGE APRICOT CANDY POPCORN

The orange juice in this recipe lends a delicious tang to the apricots and popcorn, making this an excellent and healthy snack for lunch boxes.

INGREDIENTS

- 2 servings popped popcorn
- 100 g (3½ oz) finely chopped dried apricots
- 150 ml (5 fl oz) orange juice
- 250 g (9 oz) sugar
- 2 tablespoons glucose syrup
- Finely grated rind of 1 orange

METHOD

Line 2 large baking trays with nonstick baking paper. Place the popcorn and apricots in a large bowl, stir to combine, and set aside.

In a large pan, heat the orange juice, sugar, glucose syrup and orange rind over a gentle heat, stirring until the sugar has dissolved. Increase the heat to medium-high and boil until the syrup reaches the temperature of 140° C (280° F) on a sugar thermometer. Remove the syrup from the heat and pour over the popcorn and apricots. Stir gently to combine. Transfer to the paper-lined baking trays and set aside to cool before serving. Can be stored for up to 4 days.

Makes 2 medium servings.

TIP

Keep the orange rind, but use pineapple juice instead of orange juice, and add 50 g (1¾ oz) flaked almonds to the mixture.

TOFFEE-APPLE AND CINNAMON POPCORN

Toffee apples remind me of county fairs and a once-a-year childhood treat. Using a fresh toffee-apple sauce to coat the popcorn sweetly revives that memory.

INGREDIENTS
- 2 servings popped popcorn
- 4 tablespoons butter
- 100 g (3½ oz) sugar
- 1 teaspoon ground cinnamon
- 2 large eating apples, peeled, cored and diced

METHOD
Line two large baking trays with nonstick baking paper. Place the popcorn in a large bowl. Set aside.

In a large pan, over a gentle heat, melt the butter, add the sugar and cinnamon, and stir until it has dissolved. Increase the heat to medium-high and bring to a boil. Boil for 2 minutes, or until the syrup turns a light amber colour. Remove from the heat and add the diced apple. Be careful as the syrup will spit and bubble and cook the apple immediately. Stir the sauce for 1 minute, then set aside to cool slightly.

Pour the toffee-apple sauce over the popcorn. Stir gently until the popcorn is evenly coated. Transfer to the paper-lined baking trays to cool before serving. Can be stored for up to 4 days.

Makes 2 medium servings.

TIP
A few chopped walnuts and golden raisins make great additions to this recipe – stir them into the popcorn before adding the toffee-apple sauce.

CARAMEL COCONUT POPCORN

This recipe has loads of toasted coconut sprinkled over the top of a mixture of popcorn and marshmallows. Gooey and delicious!

INGREDIENTS

- 215 g (7½ oz) sweetened shredded coconut, toasted (page 9)
- 2 servings popped popcorn
- 150 g (5½ oz) butter
- 250 g (9 oz) brown sugar
- 4 tablespoons glucose syrup
- 1 teaspoon vanilla extract
- 300 g (10½ oz) marshmallows

METHOD

Prepare the toasted coconut and let it cool.

Line 2 large baking trays with nonstick baking paper. Place the popcorn in a large bowl. In a large pan, set over a gentle heat, stir together the butter, brown sugar, glucose syrup and vanilla. When the butter has melted and the sugar has dissolved, increase the heat to medium-high and bring to a boil. Boil for 1 minute, add the marshmallows, and stir until smooth. Remove from the heat, pour over the popcorn, and stir gently to combine. Spread out on the paper-lined baking trays and sprinkle with the toasted coconut. Allow to cool before serving. Can be stored for just 1 or 2 days.

Makes 2 medium servings.

STRAWBERRY CHEESECAKE POPCORN

Dry the strawberries in the oven first, for up to six hours, then add them to creamy popcorn for a sweetly inspired snack.

INGREDIENTS
- 450 g (1 lb) strawberries
- 2 servings popped popcorn
- 350 g (12 oz) sugar
- 120 ml (4 fl oz) double cream
- 120 g (4 oz) glucose syrup
- 1 tablespoon vinegar
- 1 teaspoon butter
- 1 teaspoon vanilla extract
- A few drops red food colouring (optional)

METHOD
To prepare the strawberries, gently wash them and remove the cores. Cut into 5-mm (¼-in) slices and lay out on baking trays. Dry in the oven at 60° C (135° F, gas mark 1/8) for 4 to 6 hours. Set aside to cool.

Line 2 large baking trays with nonstick baking paper.

Place the popcorn and dried strawberries in a large bowl and stir to combine. In a large pan, over a gentle heat, warm the sugar, cream, glucose syrup and vinegar, stirring until the sugar has dissolved. Increase the heat to medium-high and bring to a boil. Boil until the mixture reaches the temperature of 118° C (245° F) on a sugar thermometer. Remove from the heat and add the butter, vanilla and food colouring, if using. Pour over the popcorn and stir gently to combine. Spread out on the paper-lined baking trays and allow to cool before serving. Can be stored for up to 3 days.

Makes 2 large servings.

POPCORN PECAN STARS

*These are little heaps of caramel-coated popcorn, set on pecans,
and topped with chocolate fudge icing.*

INGREDIENTS

For the chocolate fudge icing:
- 50 g (1¾ oz) butter
- 3 tablespoons full-fat milk
- 280 g (10 oz) icing sugar, sifted
- 2 tablespoons sifted cocoa powder

- 1 tablespoon butter, plus
  extra for greasing
- 48 pecan halves
- 1 serving popped popcorn
- 400 g (14 oz) fudge, unwrapped
- 3 tablespoons single cream
- 1 tablespoon rum extract or flavouring

METHOD

To make the icing, in a small pan, over a gentle heat, melt the butter with the milk. Add the sugar and cocoa, and stir briskly until smooth and glossy. Set aside until cooled completely, stirring occasionally to prevent a skin from forming.

Lightly grease 2 large baking trays with a little butter. Arrange the pecan halves in groups of three on the greased baking trays, and place the popcorn in a large bowl. In a large pan, melt the fudge with the cream and 1 tablespoon butter, stirring frequently. Remove from the heat, stir in the rum extract, and pour over the popcorn. Stir gently until the popcorn is evenly coated.

Working quickly, spoon heaped tablespoons of caramel-coated popcorn on top of the pecan halves, until it is all used. Set aside to cool, then spread some of the chocolate icing on top of each one. Serve immediately or store for up to 4 days.

Makes 16 stars.

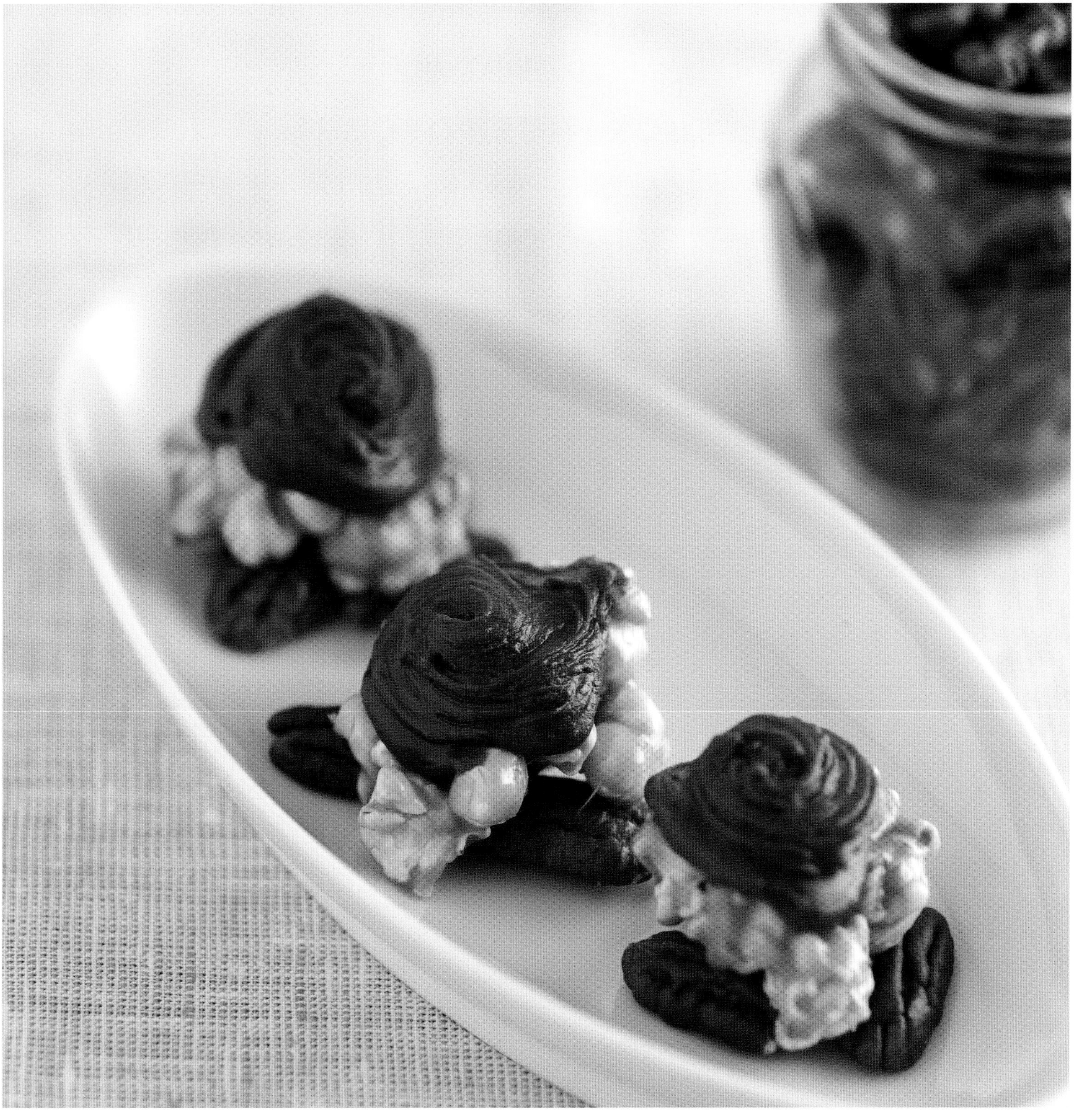

NUTTY ORANGE POPCORN

This popcorn is made with chopped mixed nuts, orange juice and grated orange zest and has a really refreshing tang. Toast the nuts before using them for the best flavour.

INGREDIENTS
- 2 servings popped popcorn
- 85 g (3 oz) chopped mixed nuts, toasted (page 9)
- 150 ml (5 fl. oz) orange juice
- 250 g (9 oz) sugar
- 2 tablespoons glucose syrup
- Finely grated rind of 1 orange

METHOD
Line 2 large baking trays with nonstick baking paper, and place the popcorn and toasted nuts in a large bowl and mix.

In a heavy pan, over a gentle heat, warm the orange juice, sugar, glucose syrup and orange rind, stirring frequently. When the sugar has dissolved, increase the heat to medium-high and bring to a boil. Boil until the temperature on a sugar thermometer reaches 140° C (280°F). Remove from the heat and pour over the popcorn. Stir gently to combine, then transfer the popcorn to the paper-lined baking trays to cool before serving. Can be stored for up to 5 days.

Makes 2 medium servings.

ALMOND MOCHA POPCORN

*Cocoa powder and instant coffee powder are a quick way to make
mocha flavouring for a crunchy popcorn and almond snack.*

INGREDIENTS

- 4 tablespoons unsalted butter, plus extra for greasing
- 2 servings popped popcorn
- 200 g (7 oz) whole almonds, skin on and toasted (page 9)
- 100 g (3½ oz) sugar
- 175 g (6 oz) glucose syrup
- 2 tablespoons cocoa powder, sifted
- 2 teaspoons instant coffee powder
- 1 teaspoon salt

METHOD

Preheat the oven to 90° C (200° F, gas mark 1/8). Lightly grease a large roasting tray with a little butter. Spread the popcorn and almonds in the roasting tray.

In a large pan, over a gentle heat, place the remaining butter with the sugar, glucose syrup, cocoa, instant coffee and salt. Stir to combine. When the sugar has dissolved and the butter has melted, increase the heat to medium-high and bring to a boil. Boil for 1 minute, pour over the popcorn, and stir gently to combine.

Bake the popcorn in the oven for 1 hour, stirring every 20 minutes to evenly coat it. Remove from the oven, stir once more, and allow to cool before serving. Can be stored for up to 1 week.

Makes 2 medium servings.

GLAZED MAPLE SESAME POPCORN

The richness of maple syrup blends beautifully with sesame seeds and cinnamon to produce a lightly caramelised popcorn snack with a delightful crunch.

INGREDIENTS
- 1 tablespoon butter, plus extra for greasing
- 2 servings popped popcorn
- 3 tablespoons sesame seeds
- 112 ml (4 fl oz) maple syrup
- 6 tablespoons brown sugar
- 1 teaspoon ground cinnamon

METHOD

Preheat the oven to 130° C (250° F, gas mark 1/2). Lightly grease 2 large baking trays with a little butter. Place popcorn in a large bowl and keep warm in the oven. Place the sesame seeds in a small dish.

In a large pan, over a gentle heat, warm the maple syrup, brown sugar and cinnamon, stirring frequently. When the sugar has dissolved, increase the heat to medium-high and bring to a boil. Boil until the syrup reaches a temperature of 130° C (250° F) on a sugar thermometer. Stir in 1 tablespoon butter and cook until the temperature reaches 140° F (280° F).

Remove the popcorn from the oven. Quickly pour on half the syrup, sprinkle with half of the sesame seeds, and mix to coat the popcorn evenly. Sprinkle on the other half of the sesame seeds and pour on the other half of the syrup. Stir again to combine. If the popcorn mixture hardens too much to mix, set it back in the oven for a couple of minutes until softened. Transfer to the greased baking trays and set aside to cool before serving. Can be stored for up to 1 week.

Makes 2 medium servings.

AMARETTO POPCORN

Macadamia nuts and Amaretto mean this one is strictly for the adults.

INGREDIENTS

- 120 g (4 oz) butter,
  plus extra for greasing
- 2 servings popped popcorn
- 120 g (4 oz) chopped macadamia nuts
- 85 g (3 oz) brown sugar
- 112 ml (4 fl oz) Amaretto liqueur

METHOD

Preheat the oven to 130° C (250° F, gas mark 1/2). Lightly grease 2 large cookie sheets with a little butter. Place the popcorn and macadamia nuts in a large bowl and stir to combine.

In a large pan, over a gentle heat, melt 120 g (4 oz) butter with the brown sugar and Amaretto, stirring frequently. When the sugar has dissolved, increase the heat to medium-high and bring to a boil. Boil for 3 minutes, remove from the heat, pour over the popcorn and nuts, and stir gently to combine.

Transfer to the baking trays and bake in the oven for 1 hour, stirring every 20 minutes, until the popcorn and nuts are evenly coated. Remove from the oven, stir once more, and leave until cool before serving. Can be stored for up to 5 days.

Makes 2 medium servings.

LIMONCELLO POPCORN

Fast to prepare, this lemon popcorn has limoncello added for extra sophistication.

INGREDIENTS
- 2 servings popped popcorn
- Finely grated rind of 1 lemon
- 1 teaspoon salt
- 3 tablespoons butter
- 1 tablespoon freshly squeezed lemon juice
- 2 tablespoons limoncello

METHOD
Place the popcorn in a large bowl, add the grated lemon rind and salt, and stir to combine. In a medium pan, over a gentle heat, melt the butter, add the lemon juice and limoncello, and stir to combine. Remove from the heat, pour the limoncello butter over the popcorn, and stir to evenly coat. Allow to cool, and either serve immediately or store for up to 4 days.

Makes 2 medium servings.

PISTACHIO MILK CHOCOLATE POPCORN

Milk chocolate makes this popcorn and pistachio treat extra creamy.

INGREDIENTS

- 75 g (2¾ oz) butter, plus extra for greasing
- 2 servings popped popcorn
- 250 g (9 oz) shelled pistachios
- 450 g (15½ oz) glucose syrup
- 400 g (14 oz) milk chocolate chips

METHOD

Preheat the oven to 150° C (300° F, gas mark 2). Lightly grease a large roasting tray with a little butter. Place the popcorn and pistachios in a large bowl and stir to combine. In a large pan, over a gentle heat, melt together the remaining butter, glucose syrup and chocolate chips, stirring frequently. When the butter and chocolate have melted, increase the heat to medium-high and bring to a boil. Immediately pour mixture over the popcorn and pistachios, and stir to combine.

Transfer to the roasting tray and bake in the oven for 45 minutes, stirring every 15 minutes to evenly coat the popcorn and pistachios in the chocolate syrup. Remove from the oven and stir gently every 10 minutes until the popcorn has cooled. Either serve immediately or store for up to 5 days.

Makes 2 medium servings.

TIP

Instead of pistachios, try adding broken-up peanut butter cookies to the mix – they go beautifully with the milk chocolate. Throw in some raisins too, if you wish.

SPARKLY POPCORN CANDY

*The freeze-dried raspberries add a bit of colour, and the sparkles
on the top add a bit of glamour.*

INGREDIENTS

- 2 servings popped popcorn
- 500-g (1 lb 2-oz) bag freeze-dried raspberries
- 350 g (12 oz) white chocolate or white chocolate chips
- Pink sugar crystals, to serve

METHOD

Line 2 large baking trays with nonstick baking paper.

Place the popcorn in a large bowl. Process the freeze-dried raspberries in a food processor until they are finely ground, and stir into the popcorn.

In a heatproof bowl set over a pan of barely simmering water, melt the white chocolate. Stir a little to prevent overheating. Pour the white chocolate over the popcorn and stir until well coated. Spread the popcorn out on the paper-lined baking trays, sprinkle with the pink sugar crystals, and allow to cool before serving. Can be stored for up to 4 days.

Makes 2 medium servings.

CHERRY BAKEWELL POPCORN

*The traditional flavours of Bakewell tart, with its delectable mixture
of almonds and cherries, transfer beautifully to popcorn.*

INGREDIENTS
- A little butter for greasing
- 2 servings popped popcorn
- 300 g (10½ oz) sugar
- 6 tablespoons glucose syrup
- ¾ teaspoon vinegar
- ½ teaspoon salt
- 1 teaspoon almond extract
- 200 g (7 oz) red glacé cherries, quartered
- 60 g (2 oz) whole blanched
  almonds, toasted (page 9)

METHOD
Lightly grease 2 large baking trays with a little butter.

Preheat the oven to 150° C (300° F, gas mark 2). Place the popcorn in a large bowl and keep warm in the oven. In a large pan, over a gentle heat, combine the sugar, glucose syrup, vinegar, salt and 400 ml (13½ fl oz) water. Bring to a boil. Boil until the syrup reaches a temperature of 130° C (250° F) on a sugar thermometer. Stir in the almond extract. Scatter the cherries and almonds over the popcorn, pour the syrup over the top, and stir gently to evenly coat everything with the syrup. Spread the popcorn on the greased baking trays and allow to cool before serving. Can be stored for up to 4 days.

Makes 2 medium servings.

COCONUT ICE POPCORN

Add the traditional taste of coconut ice to a bowl of popcorn for a pink, sugared treat.

INGREDIENTS

- 1½ servings popped popcorn
- 175 g (6 oz) sweetened flaked coconut
- 400g (13¾ oz) sugar
- 150 ml (5 fl oz) full-fat milk
- 2 tablespoons glucose syrup
- ¼ teaspoon salt
- 1 teaspoon vanilla extract
- A few drops red liquid food colouring

METHOD

Line 2 large baking trays with nonstick baking paper.

Place the popcorn in a large bowl, add the coconut, and stir gently to combine. In a large pan, stir the sugar, milk, glucose syrup and salt together over medium heat until the sugar has dissolved. Increase the heat to medium-high, bring to a boil, and boil until the temperature on a sugar thermometer registers 110° C (230° F). Remove from the heat, add the vanilla and food colouring, and stir until combined. Pour mixture over the popcorn and coconut and stir gently with a wooden spoon until they are well coated. Tip out onto the paper-lined baking trays and allow to cool before serving. Can be stored for up to 4 days.

Makes 2 medium servings.

TIP

You could change the colour of this recipe according to the season. Orange for Halloween, green for St Patrick's Day – let your imagination run wild!

INDEX

ACKNOWLEDGEMENTS

I'd like to thank Andy of Andrew James in County Durham, who supplied my popcorn maker. He is a top guy who couldn't be more helpful, and who also kindly supplied me with a halogen oven when I needed one urgently for another book. I would also like to thank Steve Lamb of MacDoctor in Winter Park, Orlando, who quickly recovered a lost chapter for me and so saved me weeks of extra work. He really knows Macs. My wonderful daughter Carly also worked with the editorial and design team to help put this book together, and they have all done an amazing job. Thanks also to my husband, friends, and neighbours, who supply their never-ending appetites as a taste team.